Structured COBOL
An Introduction

G000114672

Also from Macmillan

Advanced BASIC Scientific Subroutines
B. V. Cordingley and D. Chamund

Information Technology – A Practical Course
Harriet Harper

Microcomputer Fault-finding and Design
Robin Holland

Introduction to Computing
Percy Mett

COBOL – An Introduction
Tony Royce

A PostScript Cookbook
Barry Thomas

Structured COBOL
An Introduction

Tony Royce
North London College

MACMILLAN

© A. P. Royce 1992

All rights reserved. No reproduction, copy or transmission of this publication may be made without written permission.

No paragraph of this publication may be reproduced, copied or transmitted save with written permission or in accordance with the provisions of the Copyright, Designs and Patents Act 1988, or under the terms of any licence permitting limited copying issued by the Copyright Licensing Agency, 90 Tottenham Court Road, London W1P 9HE.

Any person who does any unauthorised act in relation to this publication may be liable to criminal prosecution and civil claims for damages.

First published 1992 by
MACMILLAN PRESS LTD
Houndmills, Basingstoke, Hampshire RG21 6XS
and London
Companies and representatives
throughout the world

ISBN 0-333-54738-1

A catalogue record for this book is available
from the British Library.

11 10 9 8 7 6 5 4 3
04 03 02 01 00 99 98 97

Printed in Hong Kong

MS-DOS is a trademark of Microsoft Corporation
UNIX is a trademark of AT&T Bell Laboratories

Contents

Preface

Acknowledgements

LESSON	SUBJECT	*page*
1.	Introduction to Computers	*1*
2.	Introduction to Computers (2)	*2*
3.	Introduction to Programming	*3*
4.	Programming in COBOL	*4*
5.	Structure of a COBOL Program	*5*
6.	Layout of a COBOL Program	*6*
7.	Vocabulary	*7*
7a.	Reserved Words (List)	*8*
8.	The Data Division	*10*
9.	The Data Division (level numbers)	*11*
10.	Revision Test	*12*
11.	The Procedure Division	*13*
12.	Introduction to Program Design	*14*
13.	Arithmetic using COMPUTE	*16*
14.	Arithmetic using ADD, SUBTRACT, MULTIPLY and DIVIDE	*17*
15.	Using Signed Numbers	*18*
16.	Using Decimal Fractions	*19*
17.	Using ROUNDED	*20*
18.	Using MOVE (1)	*21*
19.	Using MOVE (2)	*22*
20.	Revision Test	*23*
21.	Using PERFORM	*24*
22.	Program Design using Structure Diagrams (Sequences)	*25*
23.	Program Design - Coding from Structure Diagrams (Sequences)	*26*
24.	Repetition using PERFORM .. TIMES	*29*
25.	Repetition using PERFORM .. UNTIL	*30*
26.	Program Design using Structure Diagrams (Iteration)	*31*
27.	Program Design - Coding from Structure Diagrams (Iteration)	*32*
28.	Program Design using Structure Diagrams (Problems involving Iteration and Sequences)	*33*
29.	Program Design - Coding from Structure Diagrams (Problems involving Iteration and Sequences)	*36*
30.	Using IF .. ELSE (1)	*39*
31.	Using IF .. ELSE (2)	*40*
32.	Using EVALUATE (1)	*41*
33.	Using EVALUATE (2)	*42*
34.	Program Design using Structure Diagrams (Selection)	*43*

35.	Program Design - Coding from Structure Diagrams (Selection)	45
36.	Program Design using Structure Diagrams (Problems involving Sequences and Selection)	47
37.	Program Design - Coding from Structure Diagrams (Problems involving Sequences and Selection)	48
38.	Program Design using Structure Diagrams (Problems involving Sequences, Iteration and Selection)	50
39.	Program Design - Coding from Structure Diagrams (Problems involving Sequences, Iteration and Selection)	52
40.	Using In-line PERFORM	53
41.	Using PERFORM .. WITH TEST AFTER	54
42.	Revision Test	55
43.	Using Files	56
44.	File Organisation	57
45.	Storing Information on Disk using a Sequential File	59
46.	Storing Information on Disk (continued)	61
47.	Reading Information from a Sequential File	62
48.	Reading Information from a Sequential File (continued)	64
49.	Program Design for File Handling Programs - Storing Data on Disk	65
50.	Program Design for File Handling Programs - Reading Data from Disk	67
51.	Revision Test	69
52.	Review	70
53.	Worked Project 1 - Stock Report	71
54.	Suggested Programming Projects	83
55.	Using FILLER and VALUE	84
56.	Using a Printer	85
57.	Using Edited fields	86
58.	Using READ INTO and WRITE FROM	87
59.	Multiple Record Types	88
60.	Tests - Alphabetic/Alphabetic-upper/Alphabetic-lower	89
61.	Tests - Numeric/Positive/Negative/Zero	90
62.	Using AND/OR/NOT	91
63.	Expressing Conditions using Level 88	92
64.	Revision Test	93
65.	Worked Project 2 - Student Reports	94
66.	Worked Project 3 - Employee File Validation	107
67.	Worked Project 4 - Control Break	119
68.	Suggested Programming Project	130
69.	Sorting	131
70.	Using PERFORM .. VARYING	132

71.	Using Tables (Arrays) - Single Dimensional	*133*
72.	Using Tables - Single Dimensional (continued)	*134*
73.	Using Tables - Two Dimensional	*135*
74.	Using Tables - Two Dimensional (continued)	*136*
75.	Using REDEFINES	*137*
76.	Revision Test	*138*
77.	Indexed Sequential Files - Introduction	*139*
78.	Writing to an Indexed Sequential File	*140*
79.	Reading from an Indexed Sequential File	*141*
80.	Indexed Sequential Files - Reading and Writing	*142*
81.	Indexed Sequential Files - Dynamic Access	*143*
82.	Worked Project 5 - Using an Indexed Sequential File	*145*
83.	Sequential File Update	*155*
84.	Worked Project 6 - Sequential File Update	*156*
85.	Using INSPECT	*164*
86.	Reference Modification	*165*
87.	Calling Sub-programs	*166*
88.	Calling Sub-programs (2) - Passing Parameters BY CONTENT	*167*
89.	Calling Sub-programs (3) - Passing Parameters BY REFERENCE	*168*
90.	Suggested Programming Projects	*169*

Preface

This text is intended as an introduction to the COBOL(85) programming language (and program design) for students who have little or no previous programming experience.

As far as possible, the book has been arranged so that each lesson is short and covers only one topic. Easy topics are near the beginning and harder ones near the end.

It is intended that students should start practical programming exercises as soon as possible and you should be able to start writing simple programs from page 5.

There are numerous examples and exercises, and revision problems appear at intervals. Try to answer all the questions and then refresh your memory by looking back to the relevant lesson.

Six worked Programming Projects are provided. As you come to each one, try to produce the programs yourself before looking at the worked examples.

It is important to try out all the practical examples on a computer and to attempt all the exercises. Just as with any language you learn, programming languages become easy with constant use.

Acknowledgements

"COBOL is an industry language and is not the property of any company or group of companies, or of any organization or group of organizations.

No warranty, expressed or implied, is made by any contributor or by the CODASYL Programming Language Committee as to the accuracy and functioning of the programming system and language. Moreover, no responsibility is assumed by any contributor, or by the committee, in connection therewith.

The authors and copyright holders of the copyrighted material used herein

FLOW-MATIC (trademark of Sperry Rand Corporation), Programming for the UNIVAC I and II, Data Automation Systems copyrighted 1958, 1959, by Sperry Rand Corporation; IBM Commercial Translator Form No F 28-8013, copyrighted 1959 by IBM; FACT, DSI 27A5260-2760, copyrighted by Minneapolis-Honeywell

have specifically authorized the use of this material in whole or in part, in the COBOL specifications. Such authorization extends to the reproduction and use of COBOL specifications in programming manuals or similar publications."

I should like to thank colleagues and students at North London College for their help and encouragement in the development of this book.

1. Introduction to Computers

Computers come in a wide variety of sizes and types - ranging from the small home computer costing a few hundred pounds to the large machines used by banks and other large firms costing many millions.

Large computers (known as mainframes) are used to process great quantities of data very quickly - and in some cases will have several hundred or perhaps a thousand or more users - each with his/her own keyboard and screen - able to use the computer at the same time. They cost many millions of pounds, will need specially trained staff to operate them, and need to be kept in an air conditioned room. They are usually kept working 24 hours a day - with operating staff working shifts. They are used for processing bank accounts, government data, airline bookings, large firms' payrolls and for many other tasks where great quantities of data have to be dealt with in a reasonable period of time. (Consider how many cheques have to be dealt with by a major clearing bank each day!)

Medium sized computers (known as minicomputers) might have between ten and one hundred users at the same time. They are used for many jobs where the great power of the mainframe is not needed. They generally do not need a specially conditioned room - and are therefore more flexible in where they can be located. Often they might be used to serve a single building - such as carrying out stock control in a large store. Colleges and polytechnics often use them as they are reasonably powerful but much less expensive than mainframes (e.g. tens or hundreds of thousands of pounds). They still require a fairly high level of skill to manage - but are considerably simpler than mainframes.

Small computers (microcomputers) will generally fit on a desktop and have a single user at a time. They range in price from a few hundred pounds for a machine suitable for home use up to a few thousand pounds for a more powerful computer useful to a business. They are commonly used for word-processing, accounts and holding small data bases. They are however becoming very fast and powerful and gradually taking over many of the jobs which used to be carried out by larger machines.

Typically, the COBOL programmer is mainly involved with larger computers (mainframes particularly) but as smaller computers become more powerful it is now reasonably common to use COBOL on microcomputers.

Exercises
1. List 20 uses for computers in business.
2. List 20 uses for computers outside business.
3. For each of the above consider what size computer might be appropriate.
4. Name 2 manufacturers each for:
   a) mainframes b) minicomputers c) microcomputers.

2. Introduction to Computers (2)

A computer system generally consists of:

1.	the computer itself (also called the *Central Processing Unit*) - an electronic device which is able to follow a set of instructions given it in advance telling it how to do a particular job;

and

2.	a number of additional devices (called *peripherals*) which are connected to the computer and provide:

	a)	a way of giving the computer information it will need - such as a keyboard allowing it to be typed in; (these pieces of equipment are known as *input devices*);

	b)	a way of allowing the computer to give information to the user - such as a screen or a printer (*output devices*);

	and

	c)	a way of allowing the computer to store information long-term - such as a disk-drive unit (*backing-storage devices*).

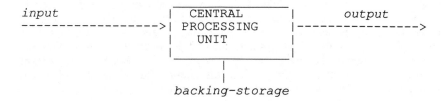

The Central Processing Unit itself consists of:

1.	the *Control Unit* - which controls the rest of the computer;
2.	the *Arithmetic and Logic Unit* - which as its name implies carries out calculations and comparisons;
3.	the *Central Memory* - which is used as temporary storage for instructions and information the computer is using at the time;
4.	a number of other devices to help the computer communicate with peripherals and work efficiently.

A computer will not operate without sets of instructions telling it what to do. These fall into two categories:

1.	instructions to carry out basic functions such as looking after filing systems on the disk, communication with the printer and handling commands from users; this set of instructions is called the *operating system* and it has to be loaded into the computer as soon as it is switched on - otherwise the machine will not be able to work efficiently;

2.	instructions to carry out particular jobs for the user - such as word processing, accounting or payroll; these are known as *applications programs* and can be loaded into the computer at any time they are needed (once the operating system has been loaded).

3.   Introduction to Programming

As has already been mentioned, the computer needs to be given a list of instructions in advance telling it how to do any job you want it to do.

So - for example - if you want it to work out the pay figures for your employees then you will have to give it a set of instructions telling it how it can do this. Likewise if you want to do word-processing on a computer - then it will have to be given a suitable set of instructions telling it how it can pretend to be a typewriter for you !

Such a set of instructions is called a *program.*

These sets of instructions can frequently be bought ready made - in the same way that you can buy a set of instructions (a recipe) telling you how to make a particular type of cake. If so then they will normally come stored on a tape or disk so that you can load them straight onto the machine and let it use them.

Often there is not a set of instructions which exactly matches what is needed. For example, a very large company which wants its computer to keep records of all its stock will probably have different requirements from those of another company so it will need a set of instructions written specially - and if so it will need to employ people (called programmers) to write these instructions.

The instructions can be written in any one or more of a number of languages designed for the purpose - e.g.
COBOL, BASIC, FORTRAN, ALGOL, C, Pascal, etc.

All these languages are similar to English or to mathematical expressions and are therefore fairly easy to learn. However they all have very small vocabularies and the main problem involved in programming is expressing a complicated task as a set of simple steps.

Most languages have specialist uses. For example FORTRAN and ALGOL are used for mathematics and scientific applications, BASIC was originally intended as a beginners' language for training (although it has since become popular for a wide range of jobs), and COBOL is intended for use in business.

The computer will not be able to follow any of these languages directly but will first have to convert anything written in them into its own language - a set of difficult-to-follow numbers - called machine code (each different type of computer can have its own machine code). This translation is carried out by a program called a *compiler* - which you would normally be able to buy to convert your chosen language to your own computer's particular machine code.

4.   Programming in COBOL

The method of writing and testing COBOL programs will vary from system to system - and you will need to look at the reference manual for your own COBOL compiler to know exactly how to do this.

In general - you will need to be able to -
1.   key in and edit the lines of instructions that you want to write;
2.   compile them (translate them to the computer's own language);
3.   set up a file containing the machine code version of the program which the computer can load from disk straight into any vacant area in its memory when required;
and then
4.   try out your instructions (i.e. run the program) to see that the computer does what you want.

Sometimes one program will allow you to do all these things - sometimes you will need a separate program to do each of these tasks - particularly an editor (or word processor), a compiler and a linker.

If you make any mistakes, they will generally show up at two points:
1.   when translating the program from COBOL into machine code (compiling) - because the compiler does not recognize something you have written (e.g. a misspelling, or incorrect punctuation);
and
2.   when running the program you may find that it does not do what you hoped it would do or simply stops.

To put right *compilation errors* - check first for simple mistakes such as leaving out full-stops or spelling words incorrectly. After that, check that what you have written is all correct COBOL grammar (compare with the examples given in the book).

When trying to put right errors which occur when trying to run your program - you have to remember that the computer will try to do exactly what you have told it to do.

Sometimes it will come across something that it finds impossible - such as trying to get information from a file that does not exist, or trying to divide by zero - in which case you will have what is called a *run-time error*. In these cases you have to alter the program as necessary or make sure that the files you told it were available for it to use are in fact on the disk.

At other times the program will work but will not do what you wanted it to do because you have given it incorrect instructions (e.g. you have told it to ADD when you meant SUBTRACT). This is called a *logic error* and will mean that you will have to alter the program.

5.   Structure of a COBOL Program

A COBOL program is made up of four *Divisions*:
1.   The IDENTIFICATION DIVISION.
This must contain the program's name - as follows:
        PROGRAM-ID. name
2.   The ENVIRONMENT DIVISION.
If the program uses peripheral devices (e.g. disk, tape, printer) - details will be shown here. Otherwise, this division will often be empty.
3.   The DATA DIVISION.
This describes the memory space needed for data the program will use.   It contains one or more SECTIONS; the most common are the FILE SECTION and the WORKING-STORAGE SECTION.
4.   The PROCEDURE DIVISION.
This contains the actual program instructions. It may be split into *Sections* and *Paragraphs* (with names given by the programmer).

Example Program

```
            IDENTIFICATION DIVISION.
            PROGRAM-ID. ADDUP.

            ENVIRONMENT DIVISION.

            DATA DIVISION.
            WORKING-STORAGE SECTION.

            01    NUMBER1    PIC 9.
            01    NUMBER2    PIC 9.
            01    ANSWER     PIC 99.

            PROCEDURE DIVISION.
            GET-NUMBERS.
                DISPLAY 'KEY IN A SINGLE-DIGIT NUMBER'
                ACCEPT NUMBER1
                DISPLAY 'KEY ANOTHER SINGLE-DIGIT NUMBER'
                ACCEPT NUMBER2.
(margin     CALCULATE-ANSWER.
7               COMPUTE ANSWER = NUMBER1 + NUMBER2.
spaces      DISPLAY-ANSWER-ON-SCREEN.
wide).          DISPLAY 'THE ANSWER IS ' ANSWER.
            FINISH-ROUTINE.
                STOP RUN.
```

Try the example program on a computer - **KEY IT IN EXACTLY AS SHOWN - taking special care over punctuation, indentation, spaces between words and after full-stops.**
Exercise
Write programs
1.   to ask for 4 single-digit numbers and print a total;
2.   to ask for a number, double it and print the answer.

6. Layout of a COBOL Program

A COBOL program would often be written down on a coding sheet (see attached example); it is necessary when doing this - and later when keying the program in to the machine - to follow certain rules:

1. Most of the program should be written between columns 12 and 72 inclusive (known as Area B).

2. All Division names and Paragraph names and certain other headings should *start* between columns 8 and 11 inclusive (known as Area A).

3. Column 7 will usually be blank but if you want the line to be treated as a *remark* - an asterisk (*) should be placed in this column.

4. Columns 1 - 6 and 73 - 80 can generally be left blank.

COBOL Coding Form

System:
Program: Example Program
Programmer:

Page no: of:
Date:

```
IDENTIFICATION DIVISION.
PROGRAM-ID. STUDENT-DETAILS.

ENVIRONMENT DIVISION.

DATA DIVISION.
WORKING-STORAGE SECTION.
01  STUDENT-NAME  PIC X(20).
01  STUDENT-MARK  PIC 9.

PROCEDURE DIVISION.
GET-DETAILS.
    DISPLAY 'WHAT IS YOUR NAME (UP TO 20 LETTERS), ?'
    ACCEPT STUDENT-NAME
    DISPLAY 'WHAT IS YOUR MARK OUT OF 5 ?'
    ACCEPT STUDENT-MARK.

PRINT-OUT-DETAILS.
    DISPLAY STUDENT-NAME
    DISPLAY STUDENT-MARK.

FINAL-PARAGRAPH.
    STOP RUN.
```

Exercise
1. Which items on the example program start in Area A ?
2. Write your answers to the exercises from lesson 5 correctly onto a COBOL coding sheet.

7.   *Vocabulary*

In COBOL, words fall into two types:
1.   words that have a special meaning - e.g. 'DISPLAY', 'ACCEPT', 'DIVISION' - these are called *Reserved Words* and may only be used for the purposes stated in the COBOL manual (refer to lesson 7a for list);
2.   words that have no special meaning in COBOL but are invented by the programmer as names for items of data, paragraphs, etc - these are called *programmer-defined words*).

Any name the programmer invents for data items, paragraphs, etc:
a)   may be up to 30 characters long;
b)   may contain any of the characters 'A' to 'Z', 'a' to 'z', '0' to '9' and '-' but must not begin or end with a '-' and must not (with some exceptions) consist solely of numbers;
c)   must not contain any spaces.

It is usual to make up names that have a clear meaning:
e.g.   EMPLOYEE-NAME, STUDENT-MATHS-MARK would be clear names for items of data, while CALCULATE-PAY and FIND-AVERAGE-MARK would be clear names for paragraphs (sections of the program).

Exercise
1.   Which of the following are allowed as programmer-defined words ? For each word that is not valid say why not.

1.	TOTAL-PAY	11.	NEW-STAFF-DETAILS
2.	WORK-OUT-TAX	12.	INTEREST
3.	GET-STAFF-DETAILS	13.	2ND-STUDENT-MARK
4.	EMPLOYEE-NAME	14.	TOTAL-COST
5.	STUDENT-TIMETABLE	15.	AVERAGE MARK
6.	DISPLAY	16.	STOP
7.	CALCULATE*INTEREST	17.	PIC
8.	NEW EMPLOYEE NAME	18.	IDENTIFICATION
9.	HOURLY-RATE	19.	DATA
10.	DIVISION	20.	WORKING-STORAGE

2.   Looking at the example programs on lessons 5 and 6:
    a)   list all the reserved words;
    b)   list all the programmer-defined words.

7a. Reserved Words

ACCEPT	ACCESS	ADD	ADVANCING
AFTER	ALL	ALPHABET	ALPHABETIC
ALPHABETIC-LOWER	ALPHABETIC-UPPER	ALPHANUMERIC	
ALPHANUMERIC-EDITED		ALTER	ALTERNATE
AND	ANY	ARE	AREA
AREAS	ASCENDING	ASSIGN	AT
AUTHOR	BEFORE	BINARY	BLANK
BLOCK	BOTTOM	BY	CALL
CANCEL	CD	CF	CH
CHARACTER	CHARACTERS	CLASS	
CLOCK-UNITS	CLOSE	COBOL	CODE
CODE-SET	COLLATING	COLUMN	COMMA
COMMUNICATION	COMP	COMPUTATIONAL	COMPUTE
CONFIGURATION	CONTAINS	CONTENT	CONTINUE
CONTROL	CONTROLS	COPY	CORR
CORRESPONDING	COUNT	CURRENCY	DATA
DATE-COMPILED	DATE-WRITTEN	DAY	DAY-OF-WEEK
DE	DEBUG-CONTENTS	DEBUG-ITEM	DEBUG-LINE
DEBUG-NAME	DEBUG-SUB-1	DEBUG-SUB-2	DEBUG-SUB-3
DEBUGGING	DECIMAL-POINT	DECLARATIVES	DEFAULT
DELETE	DELIMITED	DELIMITER	DEPENDING
DESCENDING	DESTINATION	DETAIL	DISABLE
DISPLAY	DIVIDE	DIVISION	DOWN
DUPLICATE	DUPLICATES	DYNAMIC	EGI
EBCDIC	ELSE	EMI	END
END-ADD	END-CALL	END-COMPUTE	END-DELETE
END-DIVIDE	END-EVALUATE	END-IF	
END-MULTIPLY	END-OF-PAGE	END-PERFORM	END-READ
END-RECEIVE	END-RETURN	END-REWRITE	END-SEARCH
END-START	END-STRING	END-SUBTRACT	
END-UNSTRING	END-WRITE	ENTER	
ENVIRONMENT	EOP	EQUAL	EQUALS
ERASE	ERROR	ESI	EVALUATE
EXCEPTION	EXHIBIT	EXIT	EXTEND
EXTERNAL	FALSE	FD	FILE
FILE-CONTROL	FILLER	FINAL	FIRST
FOOTING	FOR	FROM	GENERATE
GIVING	GLOBAL	GO	GREATER
GROUP	HEADING	HIGH-VALUE	HIGH-VALUES
IDENTIFICATION	IF	IN	INDEX
INDEXED	INDICATE	INITIAL	INITIALIZE
INITIATE	INPUT	INPUT-OUTPUT	INSPECT
INSTALLATION	INTO	INVALID	I-O
I-O-CONTROL	IS	JUST	JUSTIFIED
KEY	LABEL	LAST	LEADING
LEFT	LENGTH	LESS	LIMIT
LIMITS	LINAGE	LINAGE-COUNTER	LINE
LINE-COUNTER	LINES	LINKAGE	LOCALLY
LOCK	LOW-VALUE	LOW-VALUES	MEMORY
MERGE	MESSAGE	MODE	MODIFY

MOVE	MULTIPLE	MULTIPLY	NATIVE
NEGATIVE	NEXT	NO	NOT
NOTE	NUMBER	NUMERIC	
NUMERIC-EDITED	OBJECT-COMPUTER	OCCURS	OF
OFF	OMITTED	ON	ONLY
OPEN	OPTIONAL	OR	
ORGANIZATION	OTHER	OUTPUT	OVERFLOW
PACKED-DECIMAL	PADDING	PAGE	
PAGE-COUNTER	PERFORM	PF	PH
PIC	PICTURE	PLUS	POINTER
POSITION	POSITIVE	PRINTER	PRINTING
PRIOR	PROCEDURE	PROCEDURES	PROCEED
PROGRAM	PROGRAM-ID	PROTECTED	PURGE
QUEUE	QUOTE	QUOTES	RANDOM
RD	READ	REALM	RECEIVE
RECONNECT	RECORD	RECORDS	
RECORD-NAME	REDEFINES	REEL	REFERENCE
REFERENCES	RELATIVE	RELEASE	REMAINDER
REMOVAL	RENAMES	REPLACE	REPLACING
REPORT	REPORTING	REPORTS	RERUN
RESERVE	RESET	RETAINING	RETRIEVAL
RETURN	REVERSED	REWIND	REWRITE
RF	RH	RIGHT	ROUNDED
RUN	SAME	SD	SEARCH
SECTION	SECURITY	SEGMENT	
SEGMENT-LIMIT	SELECT	SEND	SENTENCE
SEPARATE	SEQUENCE	SEQUENTIAL	SET
SIGN	SIZE	SORT	SORT-MERGE
SOURCE	SOURCE-COMPUTER	SPACE	SPACES
SPECIAL-NAMES	STANDARD	STANDARD-1	STANDARD-2
START	STATUS	STOP	STORE
STRING	SUB-QUEUE-1	SUB-QUEUE-2	SUB-QUEUE-3
SUB-SCHEMA	SUBTRACT	SUM	SUPPRESS
SYMBOLIC	SYNC	SYNCHRONIZED	TABLE
TALLYING	TAPE	TENANT	TERMINAL
TERMINAL	TERMINATE	TEST	TEXT
THAN	THEN	THROUGH	THRU
TIME	TIMES	TO	TOP
TRAILING	TRUE	TYPE	UNEQUAL
UNIT	UNSTRING	UNTIL	UP
UPDATE	UPON	USAGE	USE
USING	VALUE	VALUES	VARYING
WAIT	WHEN	WITH	WITHIN
WORKING-STORAGE	WRITE	ZERO	ZEROES
ZEROS			
*	**	+	-
/	<	=	>
>=	<=		

Note that different COBOL compilers will have a different set of reserved words - consult the COBOL manual for your system for a full list.

8.   The Data Division

Each item of data that your program is going to use must be described and named - thus setting aside data storage space in Central Memory; this is done in one of the sections of the Data Division (e.g. the Working-Storage Section).

Each item of data should be given:
1.   a *level* number (dealt with in lesson 9);
2.   a *name*;
3.   a *picture* (this is a description of the item's length and type).

Numeric Data (0 - 9)
	level	data-name	picture
e.g.(1)	01	STUDENT-MARK	PIC 9.

sets aside space in central-memory for a single digit number called 'STUDENT-MARK'.

e.g.(2)   01   STUDENT-TOTAL-MARK PIC 999.
sets aside space for a three-digit number.

Alphabetic data ('A' - 'Z' plus space)
e.g.(1)   01   STUDENT-GRADE   PIC A.
sets aside space for a single alphabetic character.

e.g.(2)   01   STUDENT-GROUP-CODE PIC AAAA.
sets aside space for a 4-character alphabetic code.

Alphanumeric data (any character)
e.g.   01   ACCOUNTS-CODE   PIC XXXXX
sets aside space for a 5-character alphanumeric code.

Note that in the PIC (picture) for a data item:
         9 means that the data will be numeric;
         A means that it will be alphabetic;
         X means that it will be alphanumeric.
The number of 9's, A's or X's shows how much space has been set aside to hold the data. Alternatively, the length of the field may be placed in brackets after the type:
e.g.   01 STUDENT-NAME PIC A(20)
allows a name of up to 20 letters.

Exercise (Use level 01 for each data description)
Write data definitions for the following data items needed in a payroll program (make up data-names): employee's name, department name, employee-number (a 7-digit numeric field), annual salary (nearest pound), date-of-birth.

9. The Data Division (level numbers)

It is possible to break up an item of data into parts and refer either to the whole item or to the individual parts - e.g. EMPLOYEE-DETAILS could consist of: EMPLOYEE-NAME, EMPLOYEE-ADDRESS and EMPLOYEE-WAGE.

This can be shown using *Level Numbers*. Level 01 is used for the overall name for the data. A higher level number is used for the parts.
e.g.

```
01    EMPLOYEE-DETAILS.
      05    EMPLOYEE-NAME        PIC X(20).
      05    EMPLOYEE-ADDRESS     PIC X(40).
      05    EMPLOYEE-WAGE        PIC 9(5).
```

It is then possible - for example - to make the computer ask for the items individually   (e.g. ACCEPT EMPLOYEE-NAME, ACCEPT EMPLOYEE-ADDRESS etc.) and then display all the data using one command DISPLAY EMPLOYEE-DETAILS.

Note
1. All the data items which form part of EMPLOYEE-DETAILS are at the same level as each other.
2. It is usual to number the levels - 01, 05, 10 etc *(or sometimes 01,03,05, etc)*.
3. EMPLOYEE-DETAILS does not have a PIC statement, as it is described by the items which form its parts.

An item such as EMPLOYEE-DETAILS which is made up of several smaller items is known as a *Group Item*, while the individual items which are not broken up any further (e.g. EMPLOYEE-WAGE) are known as *Elementary Items*.

The smaller items of data may themselves be broken up into smaller parts if required - e.g. it might be useful to divide EMPLOYEE-NAME into SURNAME and FIRST-NAMES; this can be done by using another level number:

```
01    EMPLOYEE-DETAILS.
      05    EMPLOYEE-NAME.
            10    FIRST-NAMES    PIC X(10).
            10    SURNAME        PIC X(10).
      05    EMPLOYEE-ADDRESS     PIC X(40).
      05    EMPLOYEE-WAGE        PIC 9(5).
```

Exercise
Write a program to ask for a student's name, address, mark and grade - and then display all these details using a single DISPLAY command.

10.   Revision Test

1.   What are the four Divisions of a COBOL program ? (List them in the correct order). What would each one contain ?   <u>(Lesson 5)</u>

2.   Name two Sections which could appear in the third Division of a COBOL program. (Make sure that they are correctly spelled) <u>(5)</u>

3.   Where should Division names start on a COBOL coding sheet?
           <u>(6)</u>

4.   What would be meant by an asterisk (*) in column 7 of a coding sheet ?
                <u>(6)</u>

5.   In which Division should program instructions be placed ?
                <u>(5)</u>

6.   In which columns should program instructions be written ?
                <u>(6)</u>

7.   Which columns can usually be left blank ?   <u>(6)</u>

8.   Which columns are known as Area A ?   <u>(6)</u>

9.   Which columns are known as Area B ?   <u>(6)</u>

10.   What is a 'Reserved Word' ?   <u>(7)</u>

11.   What is a 'Programmer-Defined Word' ?   <u>(7)</u>

12.   What are programmer-defined words used for ?   <u>(7)</u>

13.   Which characters may usually be used to make up a programmer-defined word ?   <u>(7)</u>

14.   How long may a programmer-defined word be ?   <u>(7)</u>

15.   Give two examples of COBOL Reserved Words.   <u>(7)</u>

16.   What is meant by the symbols 'A', 'X' and '9' in descriptions of data items ?   <u>(8)</u>

17.   What is meant by a number in brackets placed after one of the symbols mentioned in 16 ?   <u>(8)</u>

18.   If a field is defined as follows -
           01   STUDENT-NAME   PIC   A(15)
      which of the following items of data could <u>not</u> be stored in it ? (In each case give a reason).
      a) Bill   b) R2D2   c) BILL   d) Anne
      e) 1001   f) John Smith   g) AAAAAAA
      h) Jonathon William Jones   i) Henry VIII <u>(8)</u>

19.   Comment on the suitability of each of the following data descriptions:

      a)   01   STAFF-NAME   PIC   X(5).
      b)   01   STAFF-ADDRESS PIC   A(50).
      c)   01   MARK-OUT-OF-TEN   PIC 999.
      d)   01   PERCENTAGE-MARK   PIC 9.
      e)   01   ANNUAL-SALARY PIC 9(3).   <u>(8)</u>

20.   Correct the errors in the following data description:
```
01    STAFF-DETAILS              PIC X(100).
      05    STAFF-NAME           PIC A(40).
            10    SURNAME        PIC A(15).
            10    FIRST-NAMES    PIC A(25).
      05    STAFF-ADDRESS        PIC X(50).    (9)
```

11. The Procedure Division

The program *instructions* are written in the Procedure Division - organised in a similar way to a book or a report written in English.

The Procedure Division may be divided into *Sections* - each with a heading; these are approximately equivalent to chapters in a book. Just as you would not generally have chapters in a short essay - a short program will not usually have sections.

The program is further divided into *paragraphs*; these would correspond to the paragraphs in an essay or report.
Each paragraph must be given a suitable heading (see lesson 7 for permissible names), and must finish with a full-stop.
Always divide your program into paragraphs (if you are using sections - then these should be split into paragraphs).

Although it is possible to divide a paragraph into sentences (and this is usual and necessary if you are using a style based on COBOL 74) each one ending with a full-stop - it is advisable not to do this if you are using the structured constructs of COBOL 85 suggested in this book, as errors can easily result unless you fully understand both programming styles.

A paragraph generally contains one or more program *statements* - each one an instruction to carry out a single task. A paragraph may, if required, be empty (i.e. just a heading).

A statement consists of one or more COBOL command words (sometimes called *Verbs*) - e.g. DISPLAY, COMPUTE, ACCEPT - together with additional information, such as datanames.

Exercise
1.   Give some examples of permitted paragraph names (see lesson 7).
2.   Give 4 examples of:
        a)   statements;
        b)   paragraphs.
3.   Give one advantage of splitting a program into headed Sections or Paragraphs.
4.   Give three examples of COBOL statements (look at the example programs on lessons 5 and 6).
5.   Place the following in the correct order (from large to small):
        statement, section, division, paragraph.

12.   *Introduction to Program Design*

When writing a report or an essay, it is helpful to make a plan - listing headings or main topics that you wish to include. In the same way, before writing a program it is useful to make a list of the main tasks that will make up your program - these tasks will probably correspond to Sections or Paragraphs of your Procedure Division.

Example
Write a program which will take data about a student (name and marks for English and Maths) then calculate an average mark and produce a report.

This program could be split into 3 main tasks:
1.   asking the user for the data and accepting it;
2.   calculating the average mark;
3.   displaying a report.

Each of these could form a separate Section or Paragraph. As the program is quite short and the three tasks quite simple, it is probably most suitable to use paragraphs -
so make up a name for each one - e.g
>   GET-STUDENT-DATA.
>   CALCULATE-AVERAGE-MARK.
>   DISPLAY-STUDENT-REPORT.

You should also think of a suitable name for a paragraph to contain the STOP RUN instruction at the end of the program - e.g.
>   FINAL-PARA.

Now fill in suitable COBOL instructions to carry out the tasks.

e.g.
```
GET-STUDENT-DATA.
    DISPLAY 'Name ?'
     ACCEPT STUDENT-NAME
    DISPLAY 'Mark for Maths ? (3 digits)'
     ACCEPT MATHS-MARK
    DISPLAY 'Mark for English? (3 digits)'
     ACCEPT ENGLISH-MARK.
CALCULATE-AVERAGE-MARK.
    COMPUTE AVERAGE-MARK =
     (MATHS-MARK + ENGLISH-MARK) / 2.
DISPLAY-REPORT.
    DISPLAY '---------------------------------------'
    DISPLAY STUDENT-NAME
    DISPLAY 'Mark for Maths:   ' MATHS-MARK
    DISPLAY 'Mark for English: ' ENGLISH-MARK
    DISPLAY 'Average Mark:     ' AVERAGE-MARK.
    DISPLAY '---------------------------------------'.
FINAL-PARA.
    STOP RUN.
```

Now decide on suitable descriptions for your data items and place them in the Data Division (it is always a good idea to group related elementary items together into suitable Group Items - see lesson 9) - e.g.

```
DATA DIVISION.
WORKING-STORAGE SECTION.
01   STUDENT-DETAILS.
        05    STUDENT-NAME    PIC   X(20).
        05    MATHS-MARK      PIC   999.
        05    ENGLISH-MARK    PIC   999.
        05    AVERAGE-MARK    PIC   999.
```

Finally, add a suitable Identification Division and Environment Division and test your program.

Exercise
1.   Complete the example program.
2.   For each of the following programs - suggest a suitable division into paragraphs - (give each paragraph a name which makes clear what it does).
     a)   Program asks for details of an employee and stores them on a disk-file.
     b)   Program reads employee-details from a tape-file, calculates pay and prints a payslip.
     c)   Program reads new-student details from a disk-file, copies them to another disk-file and prints a report.
     d)   Program reads details of a student from a disk-file, displays the information on screen, allows the user to key in changes and then writes the new data back to the disk.
3.   Going through all the stages shown in the example (and writing down each stage) design and write programs to carry out the following:
     a)   ask an employee for his/her name and annual salary, calculate weekly pay, then display a payslip;
     b)   ask a student for his name, group and exam mark (out of 10) convert the mark to a percentage and display a report;
     c)   ask a shopkeeper for the name of an item of stock, its price and how many items have been sold that week - calculate the value of the sales and display a report.

13. *Arithmetic using COMPUTE*

Data items which are going to be used in arithmetic must be stored in numeric fields. The fields declared in the Data Division must also be large enough to hold the numbers being used - be particularly careful about the length of the field that will hold the answer.

The computer can be instructed to perform arithmetic using the COMPUTE command - followed by the arithmetic expression.

e.g. COMPUTE TOTAL-WAGE = BASIC-WAGE + OVERTIME-PAY - TAX.

The sum is performed and the answer placed in TOTAL-WAGE.

The arithmetic signs are:

+	addition	-	subtraction
*	multiplication	/	division
**	exponentiation (raising to a power)		

The normal rules apply as to the order in which arithmetic operations are carried out (i.e. EXPONENTIATION is done first, followed by MULTIPLY and DIVIDE, followed by PLUS and MINUS) - e.g. -
COMPUTE X = A + B * C   means first multiply B by C and add A to the answer.

This order can be changed by using brackets () around parts of an expression which are to be calculated first - e.g.-
COMPUTE X = (A + B) * C   means first add A to B and multiply the answer by C.

NOTE THE SPACING BETWEEN WORDS AND SYMBOLS

Exercises
1.   Looking at the example program on lesson 5 - why has ANSWER been defined as two digits long ?
2.   Write programs:
      a)   to ask for a student's NAME, MATHS-MARK, ENGLISH-MARK and COMPUTING-MARK and then display his NAME and AVERAGE-MARK.
      b)   to ask for an employee's NAME and ANNUAL-PAY; calculate TAX-FOR-YEAR at 30% of pay; work out NET-ANNUAL-PAY and finally display a payslip showing NAME, GROSS-WEEKLY-PAY, TAX-FOR-WEEK and NET-WEEKLY-PAY.
      c)   to ask for an employee's NAME and WAGE; then give him an increase of 20% and print out the NAME and NEW-WAGE.
      d)   to ask for the figure for the TOTAL-BONUS to be divided among staff, and the NUMBER-OF-STAFF; then display the amount of BONUS-FOR-EACH-EMPLOYEE.
      e)   to ask for the LENGTH and WIDTH of a room; then calculate the FLOOR-AREA and display all the room's measurements.

14. Arithmetic using ADD, SUBTRACT, MULTIPLY and DIVIDE

Another method of doing arithmetic in COBOL is to use the commands: ADD, SUBTRACT, DIVIDE and MULTIPLY.

1. ADD
e.g. (1) ADD OVERTIME-PAY TO TOTAL-PAY.
OVERTIME-PAY is added to whatever number is already in TOTAL-PAY.
e.g. (2) ADD OVERTIME-PAY BASIC-PAY GIVING TOTAL-PAY.
> *(May also be written as*
> *ADD OVERTIME-PAY TO BASIC PAY GIVING TOTAL-PAY).*
The values of OVERTIME-PAY and BASIC-PAY are added and the result is stored in TOTAL-PAY without changing other items.

2. SUBTRACT
e.g. (1) SUBTRACT TAX FROM TOTAL-PAY.
TAX is deducted from whatever value is stored in TOTAL-PAY.
e.g. (2) SUBTRACT TAX FROM GROSS-PAY GIVING NET-PAY.
TAX is taken from GROSS-PAY and the answer stored in NET-PAY. (Note - the value of GROSS-PAY is not altered).

3. MULTIPLY
e.g. (1) MULTIPLY NUMBER1 BY NUMBER2.
The result will overwrite the contents of NUMBER2.
e.g. (2) MULTIPLY HOURLY-RATE BY 2 GIVING OVERTIME-RATE.
The result is stored in OVERTIME-RATE without changing other items.

4. DIVIDE
e.g. (1) DIVIDE NUMBER1 INTO NUMBER2.
The result overwrites NUMBER2.
e.g. (2) DIVIDE NUMBER-OF-STAFF INTO TOTAL-BONUS
                                         GIVING STAFF-BONUS
e.g. (3) DIVIDE TOTAL-BONUS BY NUMBER-OF-STAFF
                                         GIVING STAFF-BONUS
The result is placed in STAFF-BONUS without change to the other data items.

DIVIDE ... REMAINDER
The computer can also be asked to give a whole number and a remainder as the answer to a division if appropriate.
e.g. (1) DIVIDE NO-OF-CHILDREN INTO NO-OF-SWEETS
                       GIVING NO-OF-SWEETS-PER-CHILD
                       REMAINDER SWEETS-LEFT-OVER.

e.g. (2) DIVIDE NO-OF-SWEETS BY NO-OF-CHILDREN
                       GIVING NO-OF-SWEETS-PER-CHILD
                       REMAINDER SWEETS LEFT-OVER.

Exercise
Repeat the questions in Lesson 13 using the commands ADD, SUBTRACT, MULTIPLY and DIVIDE instead of COMPUTE.

15. *Using Signed Numbers*

If a numeric data item can be negative - it must be described in the DATA DIVISION as *signed* - otherwise the computer will assume it is always positive.

For example a data item called BANK-BALANCE is to hold a 6 digit number which may be positive (i.e. in credit) or negative (i.e. overdrawn).

The item may be declared as:

01 BANK-BALANCE PIC S9(6).

This will mean that the sign ('+' OR '-') takes up no extra space - it shares a character of storage with one of the numeric digits. So the length of this field is 6 characters.

The computer can use a number stored in the above format for arithmetic, etc - but it is not suitable for numbers which are to be accepted from the keyboard or displayed on the screen; these should be declared as follows:

01 BANK-BALANCE PIC S9(6) SIGN IS LEADING SEPARATE.

In this case, the sign takes up a separate character and will be displayed on the screen together with the number (e.g. +001000 or -023500) and must be typed on the keyboard in the same way.

(SIGN IS TRAILING SEPARATE may be used if you wish the sign to be keyed in or displayed at the end of the number).

Exercises
1.   Write data declarations for the following fields:
        a)   TAX (6 digits - positive if tax is due, negative if a tax-refund is due);
        b)   TOTAL-ADJUSTMENTS-TO-PAY (5 digits - positive for an addition to salary, negative for a deduction).
2.   Write a program which will ask for a pair of signed numbers, add them together and display the answer. Make sure your program will deal with various combinations of positive and negative numbers.
3.   Write a program to carry out the following task.
        For each credit-customer of a mail-order firm, the computer should ask for: name, address, account number, and account balance. If the account is 'in the red' the computer should display a statement for the customer stating the amount due; if the account is in credit (or zero) an addressed label should be displayed for a catalogue and order form to be sent out.

16. *Using Decimal Fractions*

If a numeric data item can contain decimal fractions - it must be suitably defined in the Data Division - otherwise only whole numbers will be allowed.
If the item will be used in arithmetic, the position of the decimal point will usually be shown by a '**V**'.

e.g.   01   WAGE   PIC   999V99.   (or PIC 9(3)V99)

Note that the decimal point is not stored and therefore does not take up any space in memory - the computer simply takes note of where the point should go so that it can be used in calculations. For this reason, on some computer systems - when entering a number from the keyboard into such a field - the decimal point is not typed: e.g. 323.95 should be keyed as 32395. Similarly, the decimal point will not be displayed in any number output to the screen - so the user has to remember where it should go.

If you want the decimal point to be displayed - it may be declared as '.'.

e.g.   01   WAGE-FOR-DISPLAY   PIC   999.99.

In this case, the decimal point takes up a character of storage - so the above data item is 6 characters long.

Arithmetic may *not* be performed on a field defined in this way (as it is not a numeric field but a 'numeric-edited' field - i.e. a field which has been edited for display purposes) but it can be used for the answer to a calculation (e.g. after GIVING) - or a number may be MOVEd from a numeric field to a numeric-edited field ready for display.

Exercises
1.   Write data definitions for the following fields (which are to be used in arithmetic):
       a)   ANNUAL SALARY (7 digits including pence);
       b)   FLOOR-AREA   (maximum size 5000 square feet and the figure will contain one decimal place).
       Now write suitable definitions if these fields are to be displayed on the screen with the decimal point shown.
2.   Write a program which will accept 2 numbers - each 5 digits including 1 decimal place - add them together and display the answer:
       a)   with the decimal point assumed (i.e. not actually displayed);
       and
       b)   with the decimal point displayed.
3.   Write a program which will accept an employee's annual salary (maximum is £20000 per annum) then calculate and display the weekly wage in the form - for example - 300.25.

17.   Using ROUNDED

Generally, if the answer to a calculation cannot be accurately stored in the field set aside for it, then it will be truncated.

e.g.(1) Suppose the following fields are defined:

```
01    NUMBER1    PIC    999.
01    NUMBER2    PIC    999.
01    ANSWER     PIC    999.
```

If NUMBER1 contains 029 and NUMBER2 contains 010, the statement DIVIDE NUMBER1 BY NUMBER2 GIVING ANSWER should result in 2.9 - however, as there is no space for the decimal fraction, this will be truncated to 2.

If the statement is amended to DIVIDE NUMBER1 BY NUMBER2 GIVING ANSWER ROUNDED, then the answer will be rounded off to 3 (which is nearer the accurate answer).

COMPUTE ANSWER ROUNDED = NUMBER1 / NUMBER2 will have the same result.

e.g.(2) Suppose the following fields are defined:

```
01    NUMBER1    PIC    9V9.
01    NUMBER2    PIC    9V9.
01    ANSWER     PIC    9V9.
```

If NUMBER1 contains 0.3 and NUMBER2 contains 0.6, then the statement MULTIPLY NUMBER1 BY NUMBER2 should result in the answer 0.18. However, there is insufficient space to hold this accurately so it will be truncated to 0.1.

If the statement is amended to MULTIPLY NUMBER1 BY NUMBER2 GIVING ANSWER ROUNDED, then the answer will be rounded off to 0.2 (which is nearer 0.18)

ROUNDED can be used with any arithmetic operation.

Exercises
Suppose the following data definitions:
```
01    NUM1       PIC    999.
01    NUM2       PIC    999.
01    NUM3       PIC    999.
01    NUM4       PIC    999V9.
```
Calculate the result of each of the following if NUM1 = 039, NUM2 = 010.
a)   DIVIDE NUM1 BY NUM2 GIVING NUM3.
b)   DIVIDE NUM1 BY NUM2 GIVING NUM4.
c)   DIVIDE NUM1 BY NUM2 GIVING NUM3 ROUNDED.

18.   *Using MOVE (1)*

MOVE can be used to *copy* the contents of one memory location to another - or to move a particular value to a location.

e.g.(1)   DISPLAY 'EMPLOYEE'S WAGE IS AT PRESENT ' WAGE
              DISPLAY 'WHAT IS EMPLOYEE'S NEW WAGE ?'
              ACCEPT NEW-WAGE
              MOVE NEW-WAGE TO WAGE.

(Displays present wage on screen, asks for new wage and then brings WAGE up to date).

e.g.(2)   MOVE 20 TO NUMBER-OF-STUDENTS.

(Makes NUMBER-OF-STUDENTS equal 20).

e.g.(3)   MOVE 'A & B COMPUTERS' TO NAME-OF-FIRM.

(Note the speech marks around an alphanumeric value).

It is important - when moving data from one field to another - to make sure that the movement is allowed. For example - alphabetic data cannot be moved to a numeric field (or vice versa).
It is also necessary to ensure that the data will fit into the field to which it is being copied - otherwise part of it will be lost.

Exercise
1.   Write statements to carry out the following:
        a)   make WAGE equal 8000;
        b)   make BONUS equal 100;
        c)   make PAY equal WAGE;
        d)   fill location AGREED with the word 'YES';
        e)   make STUDENT-MARK equal 0.
2.   Write a program that will ask for an employee's name and wage and store the data in a Central Memory area whose overall-name is OLD-STAFF-RECORD (see lesson 9); then copy it to another area called NEW-STAFF-RECORD, add 10% to the wage and display the new information.
3.   Write a program which will ask for a student's name and subject studied, and store it in a data item whose overall name is STUDENT-RECORD; then copy the data to a data item called EXAM-CANDIDATE-RECORD and display it.

19.   Using MOVE (2)

When copying data from a field of one size to one of a different size, it is important to be aware of how this is done - as you could end up losing data.

1. Alphabetic and Alphanumeric fields

Data is copied one character at a time working from the left of the field to the right: if there is insufficient space in the field to which you are copying - then the righthand characters are lost; if there is too much space the remainder of the field is filled with spaces.

e.g.   MOVE NAME1 TO NAME2
where NAME1 has been defined as PIC X(5) and NAME2 as PIC X(3).
If NAME1 contains | f | r | e | d | | - then after the MOVE has taken place
NAME2 will contain | f | r | e |

e.g.   MOVE NAME1 TO NAME3
where NAME3 has been defined as PIC X(7) - then after the MOVE
NAME3 will contain | f | r | e | d | | | |

2. Numeric fields

Data is copied one digit at a time moving from the right of the field: so if the receiving field (i.e. the one you are copying to) is too small then the leftmost digits are lost; if it is too large then the excess space is filled with zeroes.

e.g.   MOVE NUM1 TO NUM2
where NUM1 has been defined as PIC 9(5), NUM2 has been defined as PIC 9(3).
If NUM1 contains | 0 | 1 | 2 | 9 | 0 | - then after the MOVE has taken place
NUM2 will contain | 2 | 9 | 0 |

e.g.   MOVE NUM1 TO NUM3
where NUM3 has been defined as PIC 9(7) - then after the MOVE
NUM3 will contain | 0 | 0 | 0 | 1 | 2 | 9 | 0 |

If a numeric field contains decimal fractions then the number will be aligned around the decimal point after a MOVE and the excess digits at each end will be lost if the receiving field is too small.

e.g.   MOVE NUM1 TO NUM2
where NUM1 is defined as PIC 999V99 and NUM2 is defined as PIC 99V9.
If NUM1 contains | 2 | 3 | 1 | 3 | 2 | (i.e. 231.32) - then after the MOVE has taken place
NUM2 will contain | 3 | 1 | 3 | (i.e. 31.3)

e.g.   MOVE NUM1 TO NUM3
where NUM3 is defined as PIC 9(5)V9(3) - then after the MOVE
NUM3 will contain | 0 | 0 | 2 | 3 | 1 | 3 | 2 | 0 | (i.e. 00231.320).

20.   *Revision Test*

1.   Place the following in the correct order (from large to small) - paragraph, section, division, statement.   (lesson 11)

2.   Fill the gaps in each of the following sentences.
    a)   Each paragraph must start with a _____.
    b)   A paragraph must finish with a ____.   (11)

3.   Give an example of a paragraph containing three statements.   (11)

4.   Use ADD, SUBTRACT, MULTIPLY and DIVIDE - as necessary - to carry out the same task as the following statement:
COMPUTE ANNUAL-TAX =
  (GROSS-ANNUAL-PAY - TAX-ALLOWANCE) * 30 / 100.
(How many statements have you used in your answer?)   (13 & 14)

5.   What is the effect of GIVING in arithmetic statements ?   (14)

6.   Can TO be used in a statement using GIVING ?   (14)

7.   A field called ACCOUNT-BALANCE can contain any whole number between 10000 and -10000. Write a suitable data description.   (15)

8.   A field called PAY can contain any positive amount up to 99999.99 (pounds and pence). Write a suitable data description.   (16)

9.   A field called ADJUSTMENT-TO-PAY can contain any amount (pounds and pence) between 1000 and - 1000. Write a suitable data description.
                                                       (15 & 16)

10.   Write statements to carry out the following:
    a)   make STUDENT-GRADE equal 'Distinction'.
    b)   make STUDENT-MARK equal 90.
    c)   copy the value of STUDENT-MARK to EXAM-MARK.
    d)   make NEW-GRADE equal OLD-GRADE.
    e)   make LEAGUE-POSITION equal 2.

11.   A program's Data Division includes the following entries:
    01   STUDENT-NAME   PIC   X(10).
    01   EXAM-CANDIDATE-NAME   PIC   X(6).
    01   WAGE-1   PIC   9(5).
    01   WAGE-2   PIC 9(6).

```
STUDENT-NAME           |R|O|B|I|N|S|O|N| | |
EXAM-CANDIDATE-NAME    |J|O|N|E|S| |
WAGE-1                 |1|2|9|5|0|
WAGE-2                 |2|1|0|3|5|6|
```

Assume that for each question these fields start off filled as shown above. What will they contain after each of the following statements ? - (Draw the contents of both fields mentioned in the statement - showing clearly any spaces or zeroes).
    a)   MOVE STUDENT-NAME TO EXAM-CANDIDATE-NAME.
    b)   MOVE EXAM-CANDIDATE-NAME TO STUDENT-NAME.
    d)   MOVE WAGE-1 TO WAGE-2.
    e)   MOVE WAGE-2 TO WAGE-1.   (18 & 19)

21. Using PERFORM

Usually the Sections and Paragraphs in a program will simply be executed in the order that they appear in the Procedure Division.

Another way of organising a program's Procedure Division is to have a Section or Paragraph which controls the order in which the other Sections or Paragraphs are carried out. This is useful because -
1. a long program is made easy to follow - if you want to know what a program does without looking at the details all you have to do is look at the control paragraph;
2. paragraphs can be carried out in a different order or repeated.

One way of achieving this is to use the PERFORM command.

e.g.
```
PROCEDURE DIVISION.
MAIN-PARAGRAPH.
    PERFORM GET-STUDENT-MARKS
    PERFORM PRINT-REPORTS
    STOP RUN.

GET-STUDENT-MARKS.
    DISPLAY 'NAME ?'  ACCEPT STUDENT-NAME
    DISPLAY 'MARK ?'  ACCEPT STUDENT-MARK.

PRINT-REPORT.
    DISPLAY STUDENT-NAME
    DISPLAY STUDENT-MARK.
```

Exercises
1. Why is STOP RUN not at the end of the example program ?
2. Rewrite the example program so that it will do the same thing without using PERFORM.

For each of the following questions, write two programs:
        i.   without using PERFORM;
        ii.   using PERFORM.
3. The program asks for an employee's name, department and length of service (in years). It then calculates his/her annual pay by adding a bonus of £100 for each year of service to the basic pay of £8000. Tax is calculated at 30% of pay. Finally, a payslip is printed, showing the firm's name (A & B Computing P.L.C.), the employee's name, his/her monthly gross pay, tax for the month and monthly pay after tax.
4. The program asks for a student's name and marks for English, French, Computer Studies, Maths and Physics, calculates the average and prints a full report.

22. Program Design using Structure Diagrams (Sequences)

As described in lesson 12, it is usual to break any program down into a number of smaller tasks (corresponding to paragraphs) before writing the detailed COBOL instructions.

When using the programming style described in lesson 21 (using PERFORM), this breakdown can most clearly be shown using *Structure Diagrams*.

Example problem - Produce a Student Report.
Write a program to ask for a student's name and marks in Maths and English, calculate the average mark and display a report.

This program can be divided into a *sequence* of three main tasks:
1.   get the student's details;
2.   calculate the average mark;
3.   display the report.

The breakdown can be shown using a structure diagram as follows:

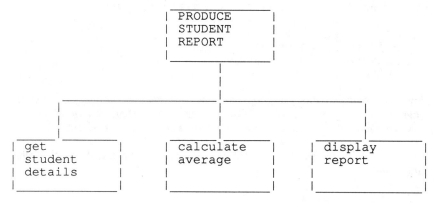

Note
1.   The overall name for the job is shown in the rectangle at the top of the diagram - the smaller tasks it splits into are shown under this in the order they are carried out (from left to right).

Exercises
1.   Produce Structure Diagrams for the exercises in lesson 12.
2.   What is meant by a sequence ?

25

23. Program Design - Coding from Structure Diagrams (Sequences)

Given a structure diagram it is very easy to write a program using the programming style shown in lesson 21 (using Perform).

Looking at the example from the previous lesson:
1.   Make up a COBOL paragraph name for each rectangle shown in the structure diagram:
e.g.
PRODUCE-STUDENT-REPORT-MAIN.
(It is helpful to call the paragraph corresponding to the top rectangle some name which indicates it is the main or overall process to be carried out).
GET-STUDENT-DETAILS.
CALCULATE-AVERAGE.
DISPLAY-REPORT.

2.   Fill the *main paragraph* with a PERFORM statement for each of the rectangles on the line immediately below the main rectangle (and joined directly to it) - three in this case.
Then add the STOP RUN statement to the end of this paragraph.
e.g.
```
PRODUCE-STUDENT-REPORT-MAIN.
    PERFORM GET-STUDENT-DETAILS
    PERFORM CALCULATE-AVERAGE
    PERFORM DISPLAY-REPORT
    STOP RUN.
```
Now, by looking at this paragraph you have a complete summary of how the program will carry out the job required. To get more detail, you would have to look at the individual paragraphs the computer is being told to perform.

3.   So, the next stage is to fill in the program statements in the other paragraphs.
e.g.
```
GET-STUDENT-DETAILS.
    DISPLAY 'NAME ?' ACCEPT STUDENT-NAME
    DISPLAY 'maths mark ?' ACCEPT MATHS-MARK
    DISPLAY 'English mark ?' ACCEPT ENGLISH-MARK.
CALCULATE-AVERAGE.
    COMPUTE AVERAGE-MARK =
        (MATHS-MARK + ENGLISH-MARK) / 2.
DISPLAY-REPORT.
    DISPLAY 'REPORT FOR ' STUDENT-NAME
    DISPLAY 'Maths mark:    ' MATHS-MARK
    DISPLAY 'English mark   ' ENGLISH-MARK
    DISPLAY 'Average mark   ' AVERAGE-MARK.
```

Exercises
1. Finish off the example program with a suitable Identification, Environment and Data Division.
2. Write a program from each of the following structure diagrams (FOLLOW THE METHOD USED IN THE ABOVE EXAMPLE).

a)

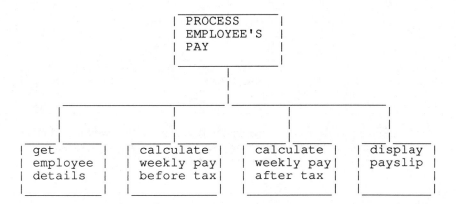

Assume that the employee details keyed in will be name and annual salary and that the payslip has to show name and weekly wage after deducting 30% tax.

b)

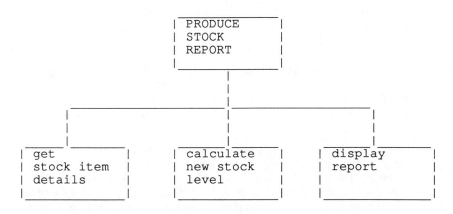

Assume that the name of the stock-item, the old stock level (number of items at the beginning of the week) and the number sold that week are keyed in. The report has to show the name of the stock-item and the new stock level.

c)

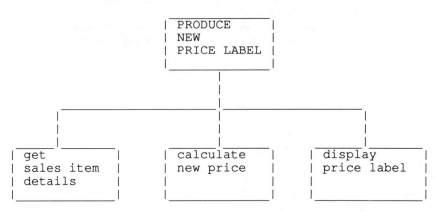

Assume that the name of the item is keyed in together with its old price. The computer has to increase the price by 20% and display a suitable label showing the name of the item and its new price.

d)

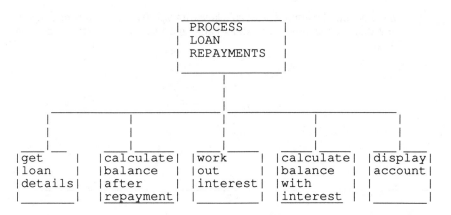

Assume that the borrower's name is keyed in - together with the amount of money outstanding from the previous month and the amount repaid this month. The computer should then calculate the new amount still owed, work out interest at 2%, and add this to the balance to produce a figure for the new amount owed - then produce an account statement showing the name, old balance, amount repaid, new balance, interest for month and new balance after interest is added.

24.   *Repetition using PERFORM..TIMES*

The computer can be instructed to repeat a certain paragraph a number of times using PERFORM .. TIMES.
e.g. PERFORM GET-STAFF-DETAILS 5 TIMES.

It is also possible to make the computer process a group of consecutive paragraphs a given number of times.
e.g. PERFORM GET-DETAILS THRU PRINT-DETAILS 5 TIMES
where GET-DETAILS is the first paragraph in the sequence and PRINT-DETAILS is the last.

Example
```
.  .  .  .  .  .  .  .  .  .  .  .  .  .  .
DATA DIVISION.
WORKING-STORAGE SECTION.
01   STAFF-DETAILS.
     05 STAFF-NAME   PIC   A(20).
     05 ANNUAL-PAY   PIC   9(5).
     05 WEEKLY-PAY   PIC   9(3).

PROCEDURE DIVISION.
MAIN.
    PERFORM GET-STAFF-DETAILS
         THRU DISPLAY-PAYSLIP
             5 TIMES
    STOP RUN.
GET-STAFF-DETAILS.
    DISPLAY 'NAME ?'  ACCEPT STAFF-NAME
    DISPLAY 'ANNUAL PAY (5 DIGITS)' ACCEPT
        ANNUAL-PAY.
CALCULATE-WEEKLY-PAY.
    DIVIDE ANNUAL-PAY BY 52 GIVING WEEKLY-PAY
DISPLAY-PAYSLIP.
    DISPLAY '*********************************'
    DISPLAY STAFF-NAME   WEEKLY-PAY
    DISPLAY '*********************************'.
```

Exercises
1.   What would happen if paragraph MAIN in the Example Program were changed to:
```
          PERFORM GET-STAFF-DETAILS 5 TIMES
          PERFORM CALCULATE-WEEKLY-PAY 5 TIMES
          PERFORM DISPLAY-PAYSLIP 5 TIMES
          STOP RUN.
```
How does this differ from the example ? Which is correct for this particular program ?
2.   Change the example program so that the computer PERFORMs a paragraph called PRODUCE-PAYSLIP 5 times; this paragraph in turn instructs the computer to carry out GET-STAFF-DETAILS, CALCULATE-WEEKLY-PAY, and DISPLAY-PAYSLIP.

25. Repetition using PERFORM..UNTIL

The computer can be instructed to repeat a paragraph - or a group of paragraphs - until a certain condition is true.

e.g.   PERFORM PROCESS-STUDENT-INFO UNTIL STUDENT-NO > 9

The computer will carry out paragraph PROCESS-STUDENT-INFO
as long as STUDENT-NO is not greater than 9.

Example

```
     . . . . . . . . . .
     DATA DIVISION.
     WORKING-STORAGE SECTION.
     01   STUDENT-INFORMATION.
          05   STUDENT-NAME   PIC X(30).
          05   ENGLISH-MARK   PIC 999.
          05   MATHS-MARK     PIC 999.
          05   AVERAGE-MARK   PIC 999.
     01   CHOICE             PIC X.
     PROCEDURE DIVISION.
     MAIN-PARA.
          MOVE 'Y' TO CHOICE
          PERFORM GET-STUDENT-DETAILS THRU
              CHECK-FOR-MORE-STUDENTS UNTIL
                  CHOICE = 'N'
          STOP RUN.
     GET-STUDENT-DETAILS.
          DISPLAY 'NAME ?'   ACCEPT STUDENT-NAME
          DISPLAY 'ENGLISH MARK ?'
                    ACCEPT ENGLISH-MARK
          DISPLAY 'MATHS MARK ?'   ACCEPT MATHS-MARK.
     CALCULATE-AVERAGE.
          COMPUTE AVERAGE-MARK =
              (ENGLISH-MARK + MATHS-MARK) / 2.
     PRINT-REPORT.
          DISPLAY STUDENT-NAME   STUDENT-NO
          DISPLAY 'AVERAGE = ' AVERAGE-MARK.
     CHECK-FOR-MORE-STUDENTS.
          DISPLAY 'ANY MORE STUDENTS ? - Y/N'
          ACCEPT CHOICE.
```

Exercises

1.   Write a program which will ask for a worker's name, hours worked and hourly rate of pay, calculate his gross weekly wage, deduct tax at 30% and print a payslip showing the gross weekly wage, tax for the week and net weekly pay - then go on to do the same for the next employee and so on until the last employee (number 19) has been processed.

2.   Write a program which will ask for a student's name and marks in three subjects, calculate the average and print a report - then ask if there are any more students on the list: carrying on to the next student if the response is 'Y' - otherwise stopping.

26. Program Design using Structure Diagrams (Iteration)

If a main job can be broken down into a single simple task repeated a number of times - this is called an *iteration* (means repetition) and it can be shown on a Structure Diagram.

Example 1 - Display a screen of 24 'hello's (in a column).
Displaying a whole screen of 'hello's breaks down into the simpler task of displaying the message line 'Hello' - repeated 24 times. On a structure diagram this is shown as:

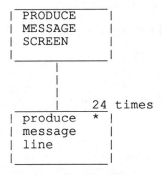

The asterisk in the top right corner of the lower rectangle indicates that the smaller task is repeated - and the number of times is shown above the rectangle.

Example 2 - Ask for a stream of numbers to be keyed in - stop when zero is typed.
This task will break down into the simpler task of programming the computer to ask for a single number - repeated until a zero is keyed.

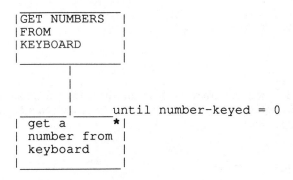

Exercises
Produce Structure Diagrams for each of the following tasks.
1. Clearing the screen consists of displaying 24 blank lines.
2. Homework consists of writing 100 lines saying 'I must work harder in class'.

31

27. *Program Design - Coding from Structure Diagrams (Iteration)*

Use the method shown in lesson 23 to turn the structure diagram into COBOL code.

1.   Make up a paragraph name corresponding to each rectangle on your diagram - giving the top rectangle a name to indicate that it is the main one.
There are two rectangles in the Example 1 structure diagram from the previous lesson - so suitable paragraph names might be:

PRODUCE-MESSAGE-SCREEN-MAIN.
and
PRODUCE-MESSAGE-LINE.

2.   Fill the main paragraph with code telling it to carry out *the task immediately below it* the required number of times - then finish off with a STOP RUN.

From the structure diagram - the main task (produce a screen of 'hello's) consists of repetitively producing a single line - so this is what needs to be said in the main paragraph. The whole job has been summarised by this statement so STOP RUN can follow.

```
DISPLAY-MESSAGE-SCREEN-MAIN.
    PERFORM DISPLAY-MESSAGE-LINE 24 TIMES
    STOP RUN.
```

3.   Fill the next paragraph with COBOL statements so that it will do the job required (i.e. display the message line 'hello').

```
DISPLAY-MESSAGE-LINE.
    DISPLAY 'HELLO'.
```

Exercise
Produce programs from the structure diagrams you produced for the previous exercises (Lesson 26). For Question 2 - make the computer display the 100 lines on the screen.

28. Program Design using Structure Diagrams (Problems involving Iteration and Sequences)

Example Problem 1 - Produce reports for a class of 20 students.
This task will break down into the simpler task of producing a report for one student - repeated 20 times. On a structure diagram this is shown as:

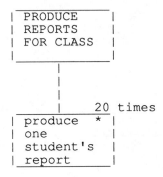

The asterisk in the top right corner of the lower rectangle indicates that the smaller task is repeated - and the number of times is shown above the rectangle.

The task of producing one student's report can itself be broken down into a *sequence* of smaller tasks as was done in lesson 22. To do this you should cover up the top box and look at the lower task as if it were the only one; so producing a report for a single student might break down into a sequence of three tasks:
1.   get name and marks;
2.   calculate average mark;
3.   display report.
These will be shown on the structure diagram by adding a sequence of 3 rectangles - so the structure diagram will now appear as:

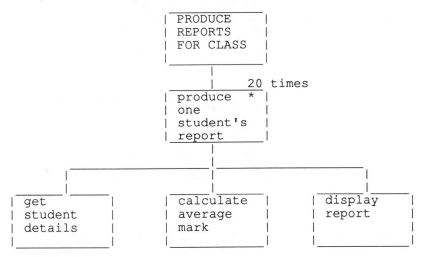

Example Problem 2 - Do bonus calculations for all employees in a firm (each employee gets a bonus of 10% of his/her annual salary).
This task will break down into the simpler task of calculating the bonus for one employee - repeated until all have been done. (The user will be asked after each employee whether he/she wishes to carry on).

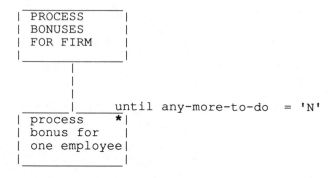

The job of processing an employee's bonus will break down into a sequence:
1.   get details;
2.   calculate bonus;
3.   produce bonus payslip;
and
4.   ask if there are any more to do.

After adding this sequence under the process-bonus-for-one-employee rectangle - the complete structure diagram will now be as shown below:

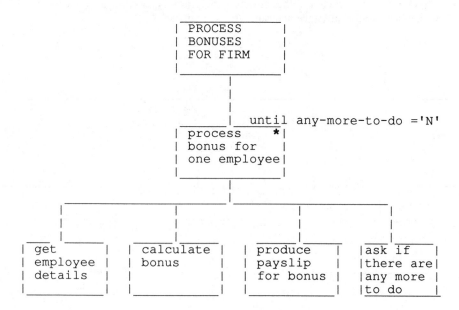

Exercises

Produce Structure Diagrams for each of the following tasks.

1. Processing the payroll for a firm consists of repeatedly dealing with one employee's pay - asking for his/her name and annual pay, calculating his/her monthly pay and producing a payslip.

    Assume that there are 15 employees in the firm.

2. Processing the stock file consists of repeatedly (for each item of stock) - asking for the stock item's name and old stock level, calculating new stock level and displaying a report.

    Ask the user if there are any more to do after each item.

29. Program Design - Coding from Structure Diagrams (Problems involving Iteration and Sequences)

Again, use the method shown in lesson 23 to turn the structure diagram into COBOL code.

Example Problem 1 - Write a program from the example structure diagram in the previous lesson.

1.   Make up a paragraph name corresponding to each rectangle on your diagram - giving the top rectangle a name to indicate that it is the main one.

Paragraph names might be:

DO-REPORTS-FOR-CLASS-MAIN.
DO-REPORT-FOR-STUDENT.
GET-STUDENT-DETAILS.
CALCULATE-AVERAGE-MARK.
DISPLAY-STUDENT-REPORT.
Compare these with the rectangles in the full structure diagram.

2.   Fill the main paragraph with code telling it to carry out *the task immediately below it* the required number of times - then finish off with a STOP RUN.
From the structure diagram - the main task (produce reports for class) consists of repetitively carrying out the job of producing a report for one student - so this is what needs to be said in the main paragraph. The whole job has been summarised by this statement so STOP RUN can follow.

```
DO-REPORTS-FOR-CLASS-MAIN.
     PERFORM DO-REPORT-FOR-STUDENT 20 TIMES
     STOP RUN.
```

3.   Fill the next paragraph with code telling it to carry out the tasks below it. From the structure diagram - the task of doing a student's report consists of carrying out the sequence of tasks below it in the structure - so the corresponding paragraph will state this:

```
DO-REPORT-FOR-STUDENT.
     PERFORM GET-STUDENT-DETAILS
     PERFORM CALCULATE-AVERAGE-MARK
     PERFORM DISPLAY-STUDENT-REPORT.
```

4.   The remaining paragraphs can then be filled in with COBOL statements:

```
GET-STUDENT-DETAILS.
     DISPLAY 'Key in name '  ACCEPT STUDENT-NAME
     DISPLAY 'Maths mark ? ' ACCEPT MATHS-MARK
     DISPLAY 'English Mark ? ' ACCEPT ENGLISH-MARK.
CALCULATE-AVERAGE-MARK.
     COMPUTE AVERAGE-MARK =
             (ENGLISH-MARK + MATHS-MARK) / 2.
```

```
DISPLAY-STUDENT-REPORT.
     DISPLAY '----------------------------------'
     DISPLAY 'REPORT FOR ' STUDENT-NAME
     DISPLAY 'Maths mark:    ' MATHS-MARK
     DISPLAY 'English mark: ' ENGLISH-MARK
     DISPLAY 'Average Mark: ' AVERAGE-MARK.
```

Note:
1.   Work down the structure diagram from top to bottom - one level at a time.
2.   In the paragraph corresponding to any rectangle, you will have a PERFORM statement for each rectangle on the line below it.

Alternative Coding

In the example it is possible, if you prefer, to miss out the DO-STUDENT-REPORT paragraph - and instead of telling the computer to perform this paragraph - change the entry in the main paragraph to read:

PERFORM GET-STUDENT-DETAILS THRU DISPLAY-STUDENT-REPORT 20 TIMES.

In this case, however, you must ensure that the paragraphs to be performed are in the right order.

You can do this whenever you have a single paragraph to be performed a number of times - which in turn instructs the computer to perform a sequence of other paragraphs.

Exercises
1.   Finish the example program.
2.   Write programs from the following structure diagrams.

a)

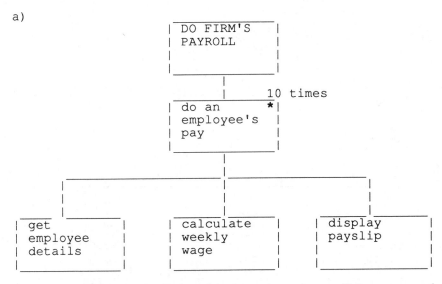

Assume that the details keyed in for each employee will be - name and annual pay. The payslip should contain the employee's name and weekly wage and have a suitable border.

b)

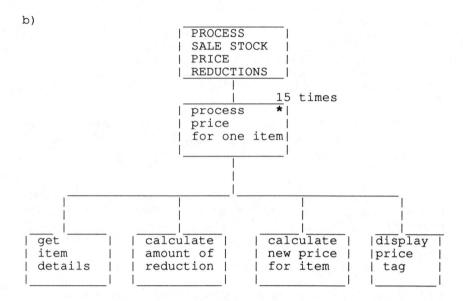

Assume that the details keyed in for each item will be - description of item, the old price and the percentage by which it is to be reduced for the sale.

The price tag should should show the old price, the amount of reduction and the new price.

c)

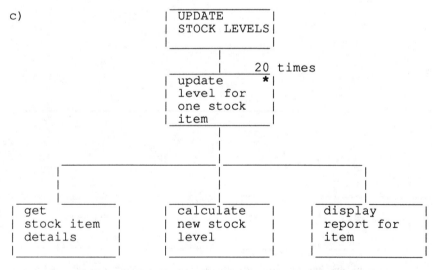

Assume that the details keyed in for each item will be - name of item, stock level at beginning of week, and amount sold for week.

The report for each item should contain the item's name, old stock level, amount sold and new stock level.

30.   Using IF .. ELSE (1)

Sometimes you might wish to program the computer to take one course of action in a certain case - and a different course of action in another case. To do this the IF .. ELSE statement is used.

For example you may wish the computer to display 'PASS' if a student gets 50 or more in an exam, and 'FAIL' if the mark is less than 50 - this could be written in COBOL as follows:

```
IF STUDENT-MARK IS NOT LESS THAN 50
THEN
        DISPLAY 'PASS'
ELSE
        DISPLAY 'FAIL'
END-IF
```

Notes
1.   The word THEN may be left out if preferred.
2.   Every IF .. ELSE statement should be finished off with an END-IF.

Sometimes the ELSE is not required:

```
e.g.   IF SALARY > 2000
       THEN
               PERFORM DEDUCT-TAX
       END-IF
```

(i.e. anyone paid 2000 or less will not pay tax - so no action is needed)

The following *Relational Operators* may be used with the IF .. ELSE statement: (the English version or the appropriate sign can be used)

IS GREATER THAN	>	IS NOT GREATER THAN	NOT >
IS LESS THAN	<	IS NOT LESS THAN	NOT <
IS EQUAL TO	=	IS NOT EQUAL TO	NOT =
IS GREATER THAN OR EQUAL TO	>=		
IS LESS THAN OR EQUAL TO	<=		

Exercises
1.   Write a program which will ask an employee for his/her length of service (in years); if the length of service is more than 5 years, the computer should display the words 'bonus payable £100' - otherwise the words 'bonus payable £20' should appear.
2.   Write a program which will ask a student for his/her marks in an exam. If the mark is less than 10, the message 'You must resit the exam' should appear, otherwise the computer should congratulate the student on his/her mark.

31.   Using IF .. ELSE (2)

Groups of statements (including further IF..ELSE statements) may be carried out following IF or ELSE commands:

```
e.g.(1)    IF MARK > 80
           THEN
                   DISPLAY 'DISTINCTION'
                   DISPLAY 'NAME PRIZE-BOOK REQUIRED'
                   ACCEPT PRIZE-REQUIRED
           ELSE
                   IF MARK > 40
                   THEN
                        DISPLAY 'PASS'
                   ELSE
                        DISPLAY 'FAIL'
                   END-IF
           END-IF
           DISPLAY MARK
```

For any mark over 80 the computer will display 'Distinction' and ask what prize the student would like; marks lower than this are divided into passes and fails.
The second END-IF indicates that the IF .. ELSE sentence has finished - so the statement DISPLAY-MARK applies to all students and every mark is printed.
NOTE THAT THE INDENTATION HAS NO EFFECT - (It just makes the program easier to understand).   THE EFFECT OF THE SENTENCE IS GOVERNED BY THE RULE - each END-IF is paired with the most recent IF that has not already been terminated.

```
e.g.(2)    IF MARK > 40
           THEN
                   DISPLAY 'PASS'
                   IF MARK > 70
                   THEN
                        DISPLAY 'GRADE A'
                   ELSE
                        DISPLAY 'GRADE B'
                   END-IF
           ELSE
                   DISPLAY 'FAIL'
           END-IF
```

Exercises
1.   In Example 2 above, what would be displayed on the screen for each of the following marks ?   a) 40   b) 41   c) 70   d) 75   e) 10   f) 60
2.   Write a COBOL sentence which will carry out the instructions in the following decision table:

CONDITIONS:				
English Mark >= 50	Y	Y	N	N
French Mark >= 50	Y	N	Y	N
ACTIONS:				
Display 'credit'	X			
Display 'pass'		X	X	
Display 'fail''				X

32.   Using EVALUATE (1)

EVALUATE may be used instead of IF..ELSE and is particularly useful whenever there is a long list of possible courses of action which could be taken depending on some value stored in a data item.

```
e.g. (1)    EVALUATE COURSE-CODE
                WHEN 1 DISPLAY 'ENGINEERING'
                WHEN 2 DISPLAY 'COMPUTER SCIENCE'
                WHEN 3 DISPLAY 'SCIENCE'
                WHEN OTHER DISPLAY 'INVALID COURSE CODE'
            END-EVALUATE
```

In the example above, the data item COURSE-CODE will be checked and action taken accordingly (i.e when course-code = 1, then 'Engineering' will be displayed, etc).

It is also possible to specify that a particular course of action will be taken if the data item is within a certain range.

```
e.g. (2)    EVALUATE STUDENT-MARK
                WHEN 85 THRU 100 DISPLAY 'DISTINCTION'
                WHEN 65 THRU 74  DISPLAY 'MERIT'
                WHEN 50 THRU 64  DISPLAY 'PASS'
                WHEN  0 THRU 49  DISPLAY 'FAIL'
            END-EVALUATE
```

This example assumes that STUDENT-MARK will always be a whole number. If the mark could be a fraction (such as 64.5 which is not included in any of the ranges above) the coding would have to be changed: e.g. WHEN 50 THRU 64.9 ..

Sometimes, the action to be taken may depend on an alphabetic or alphanumeric data item.

```
e.g. (3)    EVALUATE STUDENT-GRADE
                WHEN 'A'    DISPLAY 'DISTINCTION'
                WHEN 'B'    DISPLAY 'MERIT'
                WHEN 'C'    DISPLAY 'PASS'
                WHEN OTHER DISPLAY 'FAIL'
            END-EVALUATE
```

Exercises
Using EVALUATE
1.   Write a program which will ask a student for his/her mark (out of ten) and display 'Grade A' for a mark of 8 or more; 'Grade B' for 6 or 7; 'Grade C' for 4 or 5; 'Grade D' for any other mark.
2.   Write a program which will ask an employee to key in his/her job grade ('A', 'B', 'C' or 'D') and which will then display the appropriate wage (£500, £300, £200, £100 respectively).

33. Using EVALUATE (2)

An alternative way to use the EVALUATE statement is as follows:

```
EVALUATE TRUE
    WHEN MATHS-GRADE > ENGLISH-GRADE
         DISPLAY 'TAKE ADVANCED MATHS'
    WHEN ENGLISH-GRADE > MATHS-GRADE
         DISPLAY 'TAKE ADVANCED ENGLISH'
    WHEN ENGLISH-GRADE = MATHS-GRADE
         DISPLAY 'TAKE ADVANCED MATHS OR ENGLISH'
END-EVALUATE
```

In this case EVALUATE - instead of being followed by the name of a data item is followed by the word TRUE.

This means that the computer will check to see which condition is true - then carry out the statement which follows it.

Note that in the example above WHEN OTHER could be used instead of WHEN ENGLISH-GRADE = MATHS-GRADE - but the latter is probably clearer.

Exercises
Using EVALUATE
1.   Repeat the exercises from the previous lesson using EVALUATE TRUE.
2.   Write a program which will ask an employee for his/her length of service.
      The program should then display a bonus as follows:
      Staff with more than 5 years' service get £2000
      Staff with more than 3 years' service get £1000
      Staff with more than 1 years' service get £300
      Other staff get £100.
3.   Write a program which will ask for the names and lengths of service for
      two members of staff. The program should display the name of the
      employee who has the longer service followed by the message 'is
      promoted to manager'. If their time with the company is the same - then
      the message 'No promotions' should be displayed.

34. *Program Design using Structure Diagrams (Selection)*

If a task requires the computer to choose between two or more options - this is called a *selection*.

Example 1
The process of awarding an exam grade consists of either awarding a pass or awarding a fail.

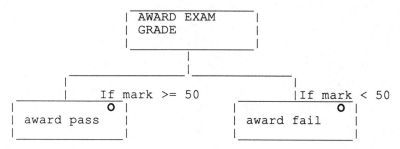

Notes:
1.   The letter 'O' in a box indicates that the task enclosed is an Option - only one of these boxes will be carried out.
2.   The condition for carrying out a particular task is shown above the relevant box.

Example 2
The task of awarding a grade consists of carrying out one of 4 options:
1.   award a Distinction;
2.   award a Merit;
3.   award a Pass;
4.   award a Fail.

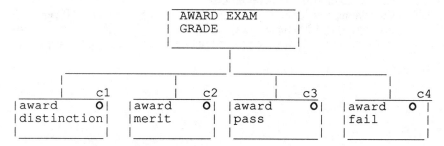

c1 - If mark is greater than or equal to 85
c2 - If mark is greater than or equal to 65 but less than 85
c3 - If mark is greater than or equal to 50 but less than 65
c4 - If mark is less than 50

Note: The abbreviation 'c' plus a number may be used for conditions rather than writing them in full above the option boxes.

Some processes consist of carrying out a particular task if a certain condition is true but doing nothing if it is not true.

Example 3
A computer has to write a letter to all customers who are overdue with payments. This can be shown as follows:

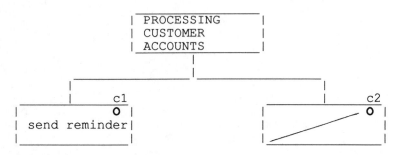

c1 - if amount-due is greater than 0
c2 - if amount-due is not greater than 0

Note:
The box for the second option contains no task as nothing has to be done if nothing is due - so a line is put through the box - meaning 'do nothing'.

Exercises
Produce structure diagrams for the following jobs.
1. Processing a student application for a course consists of printing either an acceptance letter or a rejection letter - depending upon whether the student has passed or failed 'O' level English.
2. Calculating pay for an employee consists of paying either £300 per week (managers) or £200 (other staff).
3. Processing Certificates consists of printing a Certificate if grade = 'pass' .

35. Program Design - Coding from a Structure Diagram (Selection)

Looking at Example 1 from lesson 34:
1.   Make up a paragraph name for each box in the structure diagram.
e.g.
AWARD-EXAM-GRADE.
AWARD-PASS.
AWARD-FAIL.

2.   Fill the first of these paragraphs with code stating how to choose between the options.
e.g.

```
AWARD-EXAM-GRADE.
    IF STUDENT-MARK IS NOT LESS THAN 50
    THEN
        PERFORM AWARD-PASS
    ELSE
        PERFORM AWARD-FAIL
    END-IF
```

Note that if there are two options this will turn into an IF .. ELSE statement.

3.   Fill the other paragraphs with suitable instructions.
e.g.

```
AWARD-PASS.
    MOVE 'pass' TO STUDENT-GRADE.
AWARD-FAIL.
    MOVE 'fail' TO STUDENT-GRADE.
```

Looking at Example 2 from lesson 34:
1.   As before - make up a paragraph name for each box in the structure diagram.
e.g.
AWARD-EXAM-GRADE.
AWARD-DISTINCTION.
AWARD-MERIT.
AWARD-PASS.
AWARD-FAIL.

2.   Fill the paragraph corresponding to the top box with code telling the computer how to choose which option to carry out. As there are several options, EVALUATE is probably clearer to use than IF .. ELSE.
e.g.

```
AWARD-EXAM-GRADE.
    EVALUATE STUDENT-MARK
        WHEN 85 THRU 100 PERFORM AWARD-DISTINCTION
        WHEN 65 THRU  84 PERFORM AWARD-MERIT
        WHEN 50 THRU  64 PERFORM AWARD-PASS
        WHEN  0 THRU  49 PERFORM AWARD-FAIL
    END-EVALUATE
```

This assumes that all the marks are whole numbers.

3.   Fill the remaining paragraphs with suitable statements.

e.g.
```
AWARD-DISTINCTION.
     MOVE 'distinction' to STUDENT-GRADE.
AWARD-MERIT.
     MOVE 'merit' to STUDENT-GRADE.
AWARD-PASS.
     MOVE 'pass' TO STUDENT-GRADE.
AWARD-FAIL.
     MOVE 'fail' TO STUDENT-GRADE.
```

Looking at example 3 from lesson 34:

1.   Make up a paragraph name for each box in the diagram - leaving out the box with the line through it - so only two paragraphs are needed,

e.g.

PROCESS-CUSTOMER-ACCOUNT.
DISPLAY-REMINDER.

2.   The main paragraph will contain a statement telling the computer to carry out DISPLAY-REMINDER if the account is in the red.

e.g.
```
PROCESS-CUSTOMER-ACCOUNT.
     IF AMOUNT-DUE IS GREATER THAN ZERO
     THEN
          PERFORM DISPLAY-REMINDER
     END-IF.
```

3.   The second paragraph can then be completed:
```
DISPLAY-REMINDER.
     DISPLAY CUSTOMER-NAME
     DISPLAY 'overdue account'
     DISPLAY 'Balance outstanding: ' AMOUNT-DUE.
```

Exercise

Produce programs from the structure diagrams you produced for the previous exercises (Lesson 34). For Question 1 simply make the computer display the letters on the screen.

36. Program Design - using Structure Diagrams
(Problems involving Sequences and Selection)

Example Problem - Accept the mark for a student's exam paper (out of 20), convert the mark to a percentage, award a grade (Pass for 50 or more, Merit for 65 or more, Distinction for 85 or more and Fail if below 50) and display a report.

This task breaks down into a sequence of four smaller tasks:
1.   get name and mark;
2.   calculate percentage;
3.   decide grade.
4.   display report.

So, the overall job can be represented as:

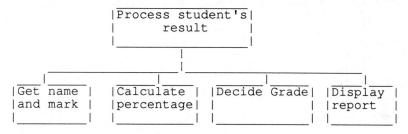

However, the third task - awarding the grade - breaks down further as it consists of making a choice between awarding a Distinction, Merit, Pass or Fail.
The whole diagram will therefore be shown as:

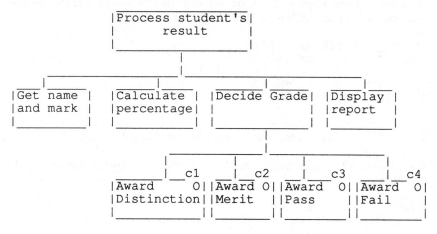

c1 - if mark is greater than or equal to 85
c2 - if mark is greater than or equal to 65 but less than 85
c3 - if mark is greater than or equal to 50 but less than 65
c4 - if mark is less than 50

37. Program Design - Coding from Structure Diagrams (Problems involving Sequences and Selection)

Use the same method as shown in previous lessons to turn the structure diagram into COBOL code.

Example Problem - Write a program from the example structure diagram in the previous lesson.

1.   Make up a paragraph name corresponding to each rectangle on your diagram - giving the top rectangle a name to indicate that it is the main one.

Paragraph names might be:

PROCESS-STUDENT-RESULT-MAIN.
GET-STUDENT-DATA.
CALCULATE-PERCENTAGE.
DECIDE-GRADE.
DISPLAY-REPORT.
AWARD-DISTINCTION.
AWARD-MERIT.
AWARD-PASS.
AWARD-FAIL.

Compare these with the rectangles in the full structure diagram.

2.   Fill the main paragraph with code telling the computer to carry out the tasks immediately below the main rectangle in the structure diagram - then finish off with STOP RUN.
From the structure diagram - the main task consists of a sequence of four smaller tasks - so this is what needs to be stated in the main paragraph.

```
PROCESS-STUDENT-RESULT-MAIN.
      PERFORM GET-STUDENT-DATA
      PERFORM CALCULATE-PERCENTAGE
      PERFORM DECIDE-GRADE
      PERFORM DISPLAY-REPORT
      STOP RUN.
```

This set of instructions in the main paragraph summarises the whole job.

3.   Now fill in the details in the individual paragraphs that are to be performed.

```
GET-STUDENT-DATA.
      DISPLAY 'Please key in mark out of 20'
      ACCEPT MARK-OUT-OF-20.

CALCULATE-PERCENTAGE.
      COMPUTE PERCENTAGE-MARK =
                MARK-OUT-OF-TWENTY * 100 / 20.
```

```
DECIDE-GRADE.
     EVALUATE PERCENTAGE-MARK
          WHEN 85 THRU 100 PERFORM AWARD-DISTINCTION
          WHEN 65 THRU  84 PERFORM AWARD-MERIT
          WHEN 50 THRU  64 PERFORM AWARD-PASS
          WHEN  0 THRU  49 PERFORM AWARD-FAIL
     END-EVALUATE.

DISPLAY-REPORT.
     DISPLAY '********************************'
     DISPLAY 'REPORT FOR ',STUDENT-NAME
     DISPLAY 'MARK = ', PERCENTAGE-MARK, '%'
     DISPLAY 'GRADE = ', STUDENT-GRADE
     DISPLAY '********************************'.
```

Now it remains to complete the paragraphs which will award the actual grade.

```
AWARD-DISTINCTION.
     MOVE 'DISTINCTION' TO STUDENT-GRADE.

AWARD-MERIT.
     MOVE 'MERIT' TO STUDENT-GRADE.

AWARD-PASS.
     MOVE 'PASS' TO STUDENT-GRADE.

AWARD-FAIL.
     MOVE 'FAIL' TO STUDENT-GRADE.
```

38. Program Design - using Structure Diagrams
(Problems involving Sequences, Iteration and Selection)

The program in the previous lesson has the disadvantage that it deals with only one student. To be more useful, it should allow the user to key in details for a number of students - producing a report for each one.

There are two ways this might be done:
1.   produce a report as each student's details is keyed in;
or
2.   allow details of every student to be entered before producing all the reports.

For the moment we shall consider the first of these possibilities.

The overall job is to process the results for the whole class and this breaks down into a repetition - processing each student's results in turn.

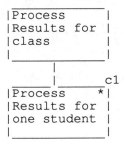

c1 - until no more students

The task of processing the results for one student will break down into a sequence - as in lesson 36 - except that at the end of processing a student, the user must be asked whether there are any more students to enter.

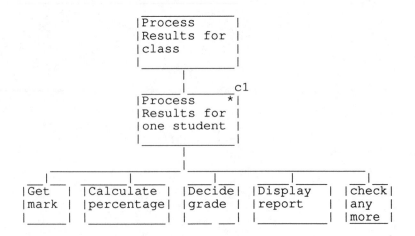

The remainder of the tasks break down exactly as in lesson 36 - so the final structure diagram will be as follows:

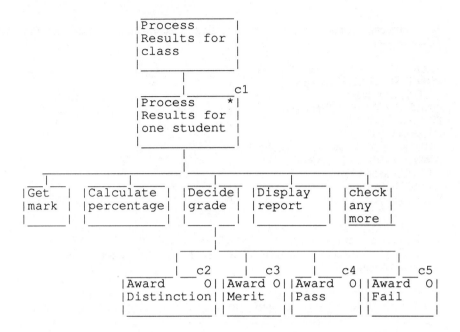

c1 - until no more students
c2 - if mark is greater than or equal to 85
c3 - if mark is greater than or equal to 65 but less than 85
c4 - if mark is greater than or equal to 50 but less than 65
c5 - if mark is less than 50

Exercises
Produce structure diagrams for the following problems.
1.   Employees in a firm are given a bonus according to their length of service:
      1 year   -   bonus £100;
      2 years   -   bonus £200;
      3 years or more   -   bonus £500.
      Your design should allow for getting information from the keyboard, making a decision and displaying the name of each member of staff and his/her bonus.
      The program should terminate when the user indicates that all employees have been dealt with.
2.   Students who get more than 90% in an exam are to be awarded a prize.
      Your design should allow for getting the data from the keyboard, making a decision and producing a report showing the name and whether or not he/she is to get a prize.
      Assume that there are 20 students in the class.

39.   Program Design - Coding from Structure Diagrams
   (Problems involving Sequences, Iteration and Selection)

1.   Invent a paragraph name corresponding to each rectangle in the Structure Diagram - e.g.

```
PROCESS-CLASS-RESULT-MAIN.
PROCESS-STUDENT-RESULT.
GET-STUDENT-DATA.
CALCULATE-PERCENTAGE.
DECIDE-GRADE.
DISPLAY-REPORT.
CHECK-IF-ANY-MORE-STUDENTS.
AWARD-DISTINCTION.
AWARD-MERIT.
AWARD-PASS.
AWARD-FAIL.
```

2.   Complete the main paragraph. Looking at the structure diagram in the previous lesson - it can be seen that **PROCESS-CLASS-RESULT-MAIN** consists of carrying out **PROCESS-STUDENT-RESULT** until there are no more student details to be entered.

```
PROCESS-CLASS-RESULT-MAIN.
     PERFORM PROCESS-STUDENT-RESULT UNTIL
          ANY-MORE-STUDENTS = 'N'
     STOP RUN.
```

3.   Processing a single student consists of a sequence of tasks - exactly similar to the program in lessons 36 and 37 - except for an additional paragraph allowing the user to state whether there are any more students to key in.

```
PROCESS-STUDENT-RESULT.
     PERFORM GET-STUDENT-DATA
     PERFORM CALCULATE-PERCENTAGE
     PERFORM DECIDE-GRADE
     PERFORM DISPLAY-REPORT
     PERFORM CHECK-IF-ANY-MORE-STUDENTS.
```

4.   Carry on working down the Structure Diagram - filling in the paragraphs with COBOL instructions. The remainder of the paragraphs are the same as those in lesson 37 except for the additonal paragraph -

```
CHECK-IF-ANY-MORE-STUDENTS.
     DISPLAY 'Any more students to enter ?'
     ACCEPT ANY-MORE-STUDENTS.
```

Exercises
Produce programs for each of the structure diagrams from the previous exercises (Lesson 38)

40.   Using In-line PERFORM

It is possible to insert a list of commands which have to be repeated between a
PERFORM..UNTIL and an END-PERFORM statement - rather than placing the
instructions in a separate paragraph.   This is called *in-line* coding - as the
computer is asked to follow the instructions (code) through in a line rather than
being told to carry out a paragraph located somewhere else in the program.

```
e.g.    PERFORM UNTIL REPLY = 'N'
            DISPLAY 'MARK OUT OF TEN ?'
            ACCEPT MARK-OUT-OF-TEN
            MULTIPLY MARK-OUT-OF-TEN BY 10 GIVING
                        PERCENTAGE
            DISPLAY PERCENTAGE
            DISPLAY 'ANY MORE MARKS TO CALCULATE ?'
            ACCEPT REPLY
        END-PERFORM
```

The same structure can be used with a PERFORM..TIMES statement.

```
e.g.    PERFORM 5 TIMES
            DISPLAY 'HELLO'
        END-PERFORM
```

The choice of whether to use an in-line PERFORM or a hierarchical structure
should depend on which is clearer in the circumstances - and on the style of
programming generally used in the firm.

The in-line PERFORM is very useful where a short set of instructions needs to be
repeated and a separate paragraph would be long-winded.

```
e.g.    MOVE SPACE TO REPLY.
        PERFORM UNTIL REPLY = 'Y' OR 'N'
            DISPLAY 'DO YOU WISH TO CONTINUE ? - Y OR N'
            ACCEPT REPLY
        END-PERFORM
```

In this case the computer will repeat the question until a valid answer ('Y' or 'N')
is typed in.

Exercises
Using an in-line PERFORM
1.   Write a program which will repeatedly ask for a number, double it and
     display the answer until a 0 is keyed in.
2.   Write a program which will ask a student for his/her course code (1, 2 and
     3 are valid course codes) and continue to ask the question until a valid
     code is keyed in.

41. Using PERFORM .. WITH TEST AFTER

Normally PERFORM .. UNTIL, etc, test the condition for finishing the repetition *before* starting to carry out the job to be performed.

It is sometimes useful to have the test at the end. This can be done using the WITH TEST AFTER command in the PERFORM statement.

e.g.(1)

```
    PERFORM WITH TEST AFTER UNTIL SEX = 'M' OR 'F'
        DISPLAY 'ENTER SEX - M OR F'
        ACCEPT SEX
    END-PERFORM
```

If the user keys in an invalid response by mistake then the routine will be repeated until a suitable letter is typed in.

The WITH TEST AFTER option can also be used when PERFORMing a paragraph.

e.g.(2)

```
PARA-1.
    PERFORM PARA-2 WITH TEST AFTER
                UNTIL SEX = 'M' OR 'F'.
    ...
    ...

PARA-2.
    DISPLAY 'ENTER SEX - M OR F'
    ACCEPT SEX.
```

Exercises

1. Why might it be advantageous to use the WITH TEST AFTER option in the above examples ? (Consider the alternative).
2. Modify each of the above examples so that either small or large letters are acceptable as the response.
3. a) Write an in-line PERFORM statement which will ask a student to key in a grade - (A, B, C are allowed), then repeat the routine if an invalid letter is typed.
    b) Include this routine as a paragraph GET-GRADE in a program which asks 5 students in turn for their name and grade.
4. Write a program which will ask a student for his/her name and mark then check if there are any more students - validating the response to be either 'Y' or 'N' - and proceeding onto the next student if the answer is 'Y'.

42. Revision Test

1. How does PERFORM work when it is followed by a paragraph name ?
    (lesson 21)
2. What is meant by a Sequence ?   (22)
3. Draw a structure diagram which shows a task which   breaks down into a sequence.
4. What COBOL commands might you use when writing the program code for a task which breaks down into a sequence ?   (23)
5. Give an example of using PERFORM .... TIMES   (24)
6. Give an example of using PERFORM .....UNTIL   (25)
7. Given the command PERFORM PARA-1 UNTIL X = 10 - will PARA-1 be carried out when X reaches 10 ?
8. What is meant by an Iteration ?   (26)
9. Give an example of a structure diagram which shows a task which breaks down into an iteration.   (26)
10. What COBOL commands might you use when writing the program code for a task which breaks down into an iteration ?   (27)
11. What is the difference between: (30)
    a)   IF X = 1
            PERFORM PARA-1
            PERFORM PARA-2
            END-IF
    and
    b)   IF X = 1
            PERFORM PARA-1
            END-IF
            PERFORM PARA-2.
    Could the way the statements are set out make the difference clearer ?
12. Explain the following command: (31)
    IF MARK < 5
     MOVE 'FAIL' TO GRADE
    ELSE
     IF MARK < 7
      MOVE 'PASS' TO GRADE
     ELSE
      MOVE 'MERIT' TO GRADE
     END-IF
    END-IF.
13. What is meant by a Selection ?   (34)
14. Give an example of a structure diagram which shows a task which breaks down into a selection.
15. What COBOL commands would you need to use when   writing the program code for a task which breaks down into a selection ?   (35)
16. Code the following using an in-line PERFORM.   (40)
    ```
    PARA-1.
         PERFORM PARA-2 5 TIMES
         STOP RUN.
    PARA-2.
         DISPLAY 'HELLO'.
    ```
17. What is an in-line PERFORM ?   (40)

43. Using Files

Any data keyed in while a program is running, is stored *temporarily* in the computer's *Central Memory* and is lost when the program finishes. If any data has to be kept for future use - it must be stored as a *file* on disk or tape; to do this, instructions have to be included in the program.

A file is a collection of information on a particular topic which has been stored for future reference.
For example, a business would need files containing:
1.   information about their staff;
2.   details of customers;
etc.

In a manual system, files might be stored in a filing cabinet, in document wallets, in box-files or in desk-drawers; a *file* might consist of a number of cards stored in a filing cabinet - each card being a *record* for a particular individual and being made up of a number of separate items of information (called *data items* or *fields*).

In a computer system, files will usually be kept on a magnetic disk or tape; a *file* is created by writing chunks of data (*records*), one-at-a-time, onto disk or tape; again, each record contains information about an individual.
So - for example - to make a file of information about all the students in a class, all the data items about a particular student would be gathered together to make a record - which would then be written onto the disk; then the same process would be repeated for the next student and so on until the file were complete.

Exercises
Details of all the students in a class are to be stored for reference.
1.   Where might they be stored in
        a)   a manual system;
        b)   a computer system ?
2.   How many records would you expect to find in the file ?
3.   What fields would you expect to find in each record ? - give them each a suitable COBOL dataname.
4.   When would the file be set up ?
5.   When might details in the file be altered ?
6.   Who might wish to refer to the details contained in the file and when ?

44. File Organisation

In order to be able to find information easily from a file, it is necessary to organise it in some way.

There are a number of different methods of organising the information in a file both as regards manual and computer filing systems.

For example, if a college needs to file student records so that information can easily be found, the information could be organised using any one of the following methods.

1. Sequential Files

Details of all the students in a class might be written one-after-the-other on a roll of paper.

In order to find a particular student's record, the roll of paper has to be unrolled until the relevant information is reached.

Note that if a new student joined the class, it would not be possible to add a new record in the correct place in the file and so it would be necessary to copy out the whole file, adding the new details in the right place when it is reached - so ending up with two files - the old list and the new one.

This sort of file organisation is called *Sequential*.

Sequential Files are perhaps the simplest type of file organisation as far as a computer is concerned.

2. Indexed Sequential Files

Another way of organising the information might be to write each student's details on separate cards and store them in a number of drawers in a filing cabinet. An index would be placed at the front of the first drawer showing where within the cabinet particular groups of cards can be found.

Any card can then be found easily and quickly without having to go through the whole cabinet.

If a new student joins a course, his/her record can be added in the right place in the file - simply by slotting in the card with others with the same index entry (e.g. same first letter for the surname).

This type of file organisation is called *Indexed Sequential*.

As far as a computer is concerned, this type of file is relatively complicated as an index has to be set up and, when the file is created, sufficient space has to be left between records to allow for later additions.

3. *Random Access Files*

It would, instead, be possible to give each student a number and place their record cards in a drawer in a filing cabinet on the basis of some calculation carried out on the number.

For example, if there were five filing cabinet drawers available, then perhaps the last digit of the student number could be taken, 1 could be added and the answer divided by 2 and the result truncated (so if the student number were 24576 - then the card would be stored in drawer 3). A calculation might be carried out on another digit of the number to decide where within the drawer the record should be placed.

It is very speedy to locate a particular piece of information as the computer can do a calculation and find the record immediately, without even having to consult an index.

If a new student joins a course, his/her record can be added in the right place in the file - simply by slotting in the card at a place determined by the calulation on the student-number.

This type of file organisation is called *Random Access*.

Again, as far as a computer is concerned, Random Access files are relatively complicated to set up, as an estimate has to be made as to how much space to leave for new records being added later.

In addition, the formula for calculating the position within the file must be carefully chosen so that records are likely to be evenly spread out - otherwise certain parts of the file will become overcrowded.

Exercises
1.   For each of the following applications consider which type of file organisation would be most suitable - giving reasons for your answer.
        a)   payroll;
        b)   airline bookings;
        c)   building society accounts;
        d)   personnel details for reference purposes;
        e)   library catalogue.
2.   Explain the advantages and disadvantages of each of the three types of file organisation mentioned above.

45. Storing Information on Disk using a Sequential File

To create a new staff-file in a manual system, the clerk must:

1.   choose which filing cabinet drawer to use for storage;
2.   decide how the file should be organised;
3.   write a file-name label;
4.   set aside desk-space for writing out the cards for the employees;
5.   open the drawer;
6.   write out cards for each employee and place them in the drawer;
and finally
7.   close the drawer.

In a computer system, the program has to go through a similar routine:

1.   choose which disk or tape will be used;
2.   state how the file should be organised;
3.   write a file-name label on the disk;

(Note that the file will usually have two names - one by which it is known in the program and another which will actually be written on the disk directory. It is important to note that the procedure for giving the file a name on the disk will vary between different operating systems, so it will be necessary to look at your particular computer's COBOL reference manual for this).

4.   set aside a space in central memory to allow each record to be filled up with data before it is written to disk;
5.   'open' the file - i.e. get it ready to use;
6.   prepare a record for each employee and write each one to disk as it is ready;
7.   close the file - i.e. state that work has finished.

Example

```
. . . . . .
ENVIRONMENT DIVISION.
INPUT-OUTPUT SECTION.
FILE-CONTROL.
      SELECT STUDENT-FILE ASSIGN TO 'STUDENTS'
      ORGANIZATION IS SEQUENTIAL.
```
This means that the file will be called STUDENTS on the disk directory. STUDENT-FILE is the temporary name by which the file is known in the program.
Note that this section of the program will vary with different computer systems - refer to the COBOL manual for your system.

```
DATA DIVISION.
FILE SECTION.
FD   STUDENT-FILE.
01   STUDENT-DETAILS-RECORD.
      05   STUDENT-NAME         PIC   X(30).
      05   STUDENT-ADDRESS      PIC   X(60).
```
This sets aside space in the Central Memory where a record can be stored temporarily until it is written onto the disk.

```
PROCEDURE DIVISION.
PROCESS-STUDENT-DATA-MAIN.
     PERFORM OPEN-FILE
     PERFORM GET-STUDENT-DETAILS
     PERFORM WRITE-TO-DISK
     PERFORM CLOSE-FILE
     STOP RUN.


OPEN-FILE.
     OPEN OUTPUT STUDENT-FILE.
```

The file has to be 'opened' ready for Output (i.e. data will be sent OUT from the computer to the disk file).

```
GET-STUDENT-DETAILS.
     DISPLAY 'NAME ? ' ACCEPT STUDENT-NAME
     DISPLAY 'ADDRESS ?' ACCEPT STUDENT-ADDRESS.
```

Places data in the record area of Central Memory ready to be written to disk.

```
WRITE-TO-DISK.
     WRITE STUDENT-DETAILS-RECORD.
```

*As each student's record is completed - it is 'written' onto the disk file; (the WRITE verb is followed by the **record name** - the computer knows from the FD entry in the Data Division which file goes with this record-name).*

```
CLOSE-FILE.
     CLOSE STUDENT-FILE.
```

Exercise

Write a program asking for the name (30 characters) and wages (5 digits) of an employee - storing the employee's record on disk in a file called 'staff'.

Generally, a file will contain a large number of records - e.g. one record for each type of stock on the shelves.
So, the program has to open the file, deal with the records one at a time (for each one, getting the data and writing the record to the file before moving on to the record for the next item) and finally close the file.

Example
. . . . .
```
ENVIRONMENT DIVISION.
INPUT-OUTPUT SECTION.
FILE-CONTROL.
      SELECT STOCK-FILE ASSIGN TO 'STOCK'
      ORGANIZATION IS SEQUENTIAL.
DATA DIVISION.
FILE SECTION.
FD STOCK-FILE.
01   STOCK-RECORD.
      05    STOCK-NUMBER  PIC 9(5).
      05    STOCK-DESCRIPTION PIC X(30).
      05    STOCK-QUANTITY PIC 9(3).
PROCEDURE DIVISION.
MAKE-STOCK-FILE-MAIN.
      PERFORM OPEN-FILE
      PERFORM PROCESS-STOCK-RECORD 5 TIMES
      PERFORM CLOSE-FILE
      STOP RUN.
OPEN-FILE.
      OPEN OUTPUT STOCK-FILE.
PROCESS-STOCK-RECORD.
      PERFORM GET-DETAILS-FROM-KEYBOARD
      PERFORM WRITE-TO-DISK.
CLOSE-FILE.
      CLOSE STOCK-FILE.
GET-DETAILS-FROM-KEYBOARD.
      DISPLAY 'Stock Number (5 digits) '
      ACCEPT STOCK-NUMBER
      DISPLAY 'Description of Item '
      ACCEPT STOCK-DESCRIPTION
      DISPLAY 'Quantity  in Stock '
      ACCEPT STOCK-QUANTITY.
WRITE-TO-DISK.
      WRITE STOCK-RECORD.
```

Exercises
1.   Write a program which will ask for the name (20 letters), and mark (3 digits) for each student in a class of twenty and save the records to disk.
2.   Write a program which will ask for the name and wage for each of five employees and save them on disk.

47. Reading Information from a Sequential File

To process the data contained in a staff-file in a manual system, the clerk has to:

1.   note which filing cabinet drawer contains the file;
2.   check the file-name label;
3.   note how the file is organised;
4.   set aside desk-space for looking at and processing each employee record card;
5.   open the drawer;
6.   read each employee's card employee and deal with the information;
and finally
7.   close the drawer.

In a computer system, the program has to go through a similar routine:

1.   note which disk or tape is being used;
2.   note the file name on the disk;
3.   note how the file is organised;
4.   set aside a space in central memory to allow each record to be processed once it has been read from the disk;
5.   'open' the file - i.e. get it ready to use;
6.   starting at the beginning of the file - go through, one-by-one, reading (and processing) each employee's record;
7.   close the file - i.e. state that work on the file has finished.

Example (to read a file called 'STUDENTS' stored on disk - previously created by the example program from lesson 42 - note that this file contained one record only).
. . . .
```
ENVIRONMENT DIVISION.
INPUT-OUTPUT SECTION.
FILE-CONTROL.
     SELECT STUDENT-FILE ASSIGN TO 'STUDENTS'
     ORGANIZATION IS SEQUENTIAL.

DATA DIVISION.
FILE SECTION.
FD   STUDENT-FILE.
01   STUDENT-RECORD.
     05     STUDENT-NAME       PIC   X(30).
     05     STUDENT-ADDRESS    PIC   X(60).

PROCEDURE DIVISION.
MAIN.
     PERFORM OPEN-FILE
     PERFORM READ-RECORD
     PERFORM PRINT-DETAILS
     PERFORM CLOSE-FILE
     STOP RUN.
```

```
OPEN-FILE.
    OPEN INPUT STUDENT-FILE.
```
The file has to be 'opened' ready to be used as Input to the computer (i.e. data will be sent IN to the computer from the disk file).

```
READ-RECORD.
    READ STUDENT-FILE
        AT END DISPLAY 'EOF'
    END-READ.
```
*The READ verb is followed by the **file name**; one record is automatically read from the file into the correct Central Memory record area as defined in the Data Division. (Contrast with the WRITE verb (Lesson 45 and 46)).*

The READ statement must include a command telling the computer what to do if it tries to read a record when it has already read the last one in the file (i.e. End of File). In this case we have simply told it to display a message.

The END-READ finishes the set of instructions associated with the READ command.

```
PRINT-DETAILS.
    DISPLAY STUDENT-NAME.
    DISPLAY STUDENT-ADDRESS.

CLOSE-FILE.
    CLOSE STUDENT-FILE.
```

Note

The program to read the file must be compatible with the program which was written to create the file (e.g. - same record length, same filename on the disk directory - i.e. the name in inverted commas).

Exercise

Write a program which will read and display the information (only one record) from the file called 'staff' created by the exercise program from lesson 45.

48. Reading Information from a Sequential File (continued)

If a file contains more than one record, then the program has to open the file, process the records one-by-one, and finally close the file.

Example

```
. . . . .
ENVIRONMENT DIVISION.
INPUT-OUTPUT SECTION.
FILE-CONTROL.
     SELECT STOCK-FILE ASSIGN TO 'STOCK'
     ORGANIZATION IS SEQUENTIAL.

DATA DIVISION.
FILE SECTION.
FD STOCK-FILE.
01  STOCK-RECORD.
     05   STOCK-NUMBER   PIC 9(5).
     05   STOCK-DESCRIPTION    PIC X(30).
     05   STOCK-QUANTITY PIC 9(3).

WORKING-STORAGE SECTION.
01   EOF-INDICATOR   PIC X   VALUE SPACES.

PROCEDURE DIVISION.
MAKE-STOCK-FILE-MAIN.
     PERFORM OPEN-FILE
     PERFORM PROCESS-STOCK-RECORD 5 TIMES
     PERFORM CLOSE-FILE
     STOP RUN.

OPEN-FILE.
     OPEN INPUT STOCK-FILE.
PROCESS-STOCK-RECORD.
     PERFORM GET-DETAILS-FROM-DISK
     PERFORM DISPLAY-DETAILS.
CLOSE-FILE.
     CLOSE STOCK-FILE.

GET-DETAILS-FROM-DISK.
     READ STOCK-FILE AT END DISPLAY 'END OF FILE'
     END-READ.
DISPLAY-DETAILS.
     DISPLAY 'Stock Number ', STOCK-NUMBER
     DISPLAY 'Description ', STOCK-DESCRIPTION
     DISPLAY 'Quantity  in Stock ', STOCK-QUANTITY.
```

Exercises
1.   Write a program which will read the student file created by your program from lesson 46, exercise (1) and display the details.
2.   Write a program which will read the staff file created by your program from lesson 46, exercise (2) and display the details.

49. *Program Design for File Handling Programs - Storing Data on Disk*

Example
Design a program which will allow information on a class of students to be keyed in and stored on disk.

Typical file handling programs involve a sequence of three main tasks:
1. open the file;
2. process the file;
3. close the file.

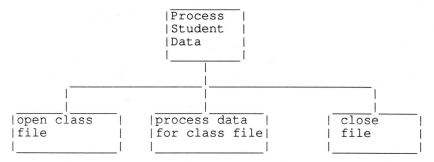

Note how this would relate to the steps in dealing with a file of information held on cards in a filing cabinet:
1. open the cabinet;
2. process the file;
3. close the cabinet.

Processing the data about the class consists of processing the data about one student, then the next and so on - i.e. a repetition.

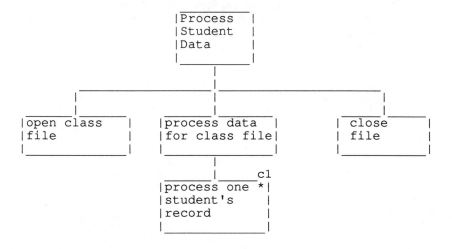

c1 - until no more students to key in

The job of processing a student's record will break down into a sequence:
1.   get details;
2.   write student's details to disk.
In addition, after dealing with each student, the user will have to be asked whether there are any more students to key in.

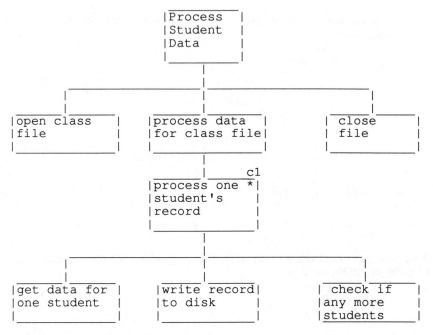

c1 - until no more students to key in

Exercises
1.   Write a COBOL program from the above structure diagram.
2.   Design and write a program which will allow names and addresses of a firm's customers to be stored on disk.

50. Program Design for File Handling Programs - Reading Data from Disk

Example Program
Design a program which will allow a file of data on a class of students to be read and displayed.

Again the main tasks are :
1.   open the file;
2.   process the data as requested;
3.   close the file.

However, the problem generally arises that you do not know whether or not a file contains any data. (In the previous lessons this problem was avoided by writing fixed numbers of records into the data files). To avoid the program trying to process nothing, it is usual to try to read a record first to check whether to go on.

So the sequence is normally carried out as follows:
1.   open the file;
2.   (try to) read a record;
3.   process the data as requested;
4.   close the file.

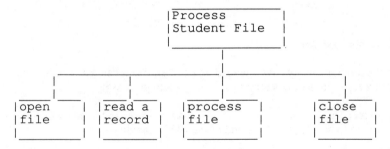

Processing the file consists of processing each individual record - a repetitive task.

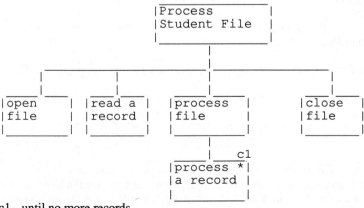

c1 - until no more records

Processing a record would generally consist of reading a record from the file and displaying it - however one record has already been read - so this can be displayed and then the next record read.

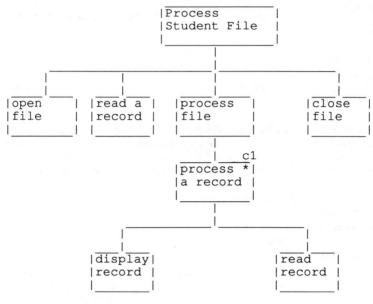

c1 - until no more records

Note that the program always has one read 'in hand' so that it can test whether the read was successful in getting a record before trying to process it.

The programmer should define a field in the Working-Storage Section which the program can use to hold a note if the end of the file is found:

e.g. 01 END-OF-FILE-INDICATOR PIC X VALUE SPACE.

```
READ STUDENT-FILE
        AT END MOVE 'E' TO END-OF-FILE-INDICATOR
END-READ
```
will then instruct the computer to move an 'E' to the field if it finds no more records in the file.

The computer can then be instructed to process records until the end of the file is reached:
PERFORM PROCESS-RECORD UNTIL END-OF-FILE-INDICATOR = 'E'.

(So condition c1 could read: until END-OF-FILE-INDICATOR = 'E').

Exercises
1.   Write a COBOL program from the above structure diagram.
2.   Design and write a program which will allow the names and addresses of a firm's customers to be read from the disk file created by the program from the exercise program in the previous lesson.

51.   Revision Test

1.   What is a) a file b) a record c) a field ? Give examples of each.
                                         (Lesson 43)
2.   What is meant by:
     a)   a *Sequential File* ?
     b)   an *Indexed Sequential File* ?
     c)   a *Random Access File* ?   (44)
3.   Discuss what sort of applications might use each of the above and why.
4.   Which type of file would take up least space on disk (for the same amount
     of data stored) ? Give a reason for your answer.   (44)
5.   Which type of file would allow the fastest access to one particular record ?
     Give a reason for your answer.   (44)
6.   Which type of file would allow the fastest production of a complete list
     showing all the information in the file? Explain your answer. (44)
8.   Would it be practical to store any of the types of file organisation
     mentioned above on magnetic tape ? Explain your answer. (44)
9.   Would it be practical to store any of the types of file mentioned above on
     magnetic disk ? Explain your answer.   (44)
10. Write a suitable ENVIRONMENT DIVISION entry which will set up a
     file to be called STOCK-FILE within the program and 'stock1' on the disk
     directory.   (45)
11. Write a suitable DATA DIVISION entry for the above file. (45)
12. Write statements to do the following:
     a)   open the file to receive information. (45)
     b)   send a record to the file.   (45)
     c)   open the file so that data can be read from it. (47)
     d)   read a record from the file.   (47)
13. Which parts of a file-handling program are likely to vary if the program is
     to be used on another computer system.   (45)
14. Why is it usual to do a *read-ahead* (i.e. read one record before starting the
     main processing of the file) ? - Give two reasons.   (50)
15. Change one of the file-reading programs you wrote for Lesson 50 so that
     there is no read-ahead. What happens when it is run ? Explain why.

52. *Review*

1.   What are: *Reserved Words, Programmer-Defined Words.*
     Give 10 examples of each.
     Explain what goes to make a valid Programmer Defined Word *(e.g. length, type of characters allowed).*
2.   What does PIC stand for ? Explain its purpose.
3.   Explain the terms: *elementary item, group item.* Give 5 examples of each.
4.   Explain the difference between the following:
     a)   DISPLAY STUDENT-DETAILS.
     b)   DISPLAY 'STUDENT DETAILS'.
5.   Explain the following terms: *record, file, field* ? Use examples in your explanation.
6.   What sort of characters could be stored in a field defined as PIC 9 ?
7.   What sort of characters could be stored in a field defined as PIC X ?
8.   What sort of characters could be stored in a field defined as PIC A ?
9.   Write a suitable statement which will open STUDENT-FILE ready for reading.
10. Write a suitable statement which will open STUDENT-FILE ready for writing.
11. Write a suitable ENVIRONMENT DIVISION for a program which uses two Sequential Files - called OLD-MAIN-FILE and NEW-MAIN-FILE within the program and *staff1* and *staff2* respectively on the disk directory.
12. Given the following Data Division entry:
     FD   STUDENT-FILE.
     01   STUDENT-RECORD   PIC   X(50).
     a)   write a suitable statement which will write to disk any information temporarily stored in STUDENT-RECORD.
     b)   write a suitable statement to read information from the file. Where will the computer place the data when it has been read ?
13. DATA-ITEM-1 is defined as PIC X(4) VALUE 'WORK'
     and
     DATA-ITEM-2 is defined as PIC X(5) VALUE 'SHEEP'
     what will be the effect of each of the following statements ?
     a)   MOVE DATA-ITEM-1 TO DATA-ITEM-2
     b)   MOVE DATA-ITEM-2 TO DATA-ITEM-1.
14. Explain the effect of the following:
     MOVE 'HELLO' TO GREETING.
     Write a suitable Data Division entry for GREETING.
15. What is the purpose of GIVING in an arithmetic statement ? Give 5 examples of its use.
16. Give an example of a *Relational Operator.*
17. What command indicates the end of a COBOL program ?
18. Why is it a good idea to design a program before writing it ?
19. How do you indicate that a line is intended as a comment and not to be compiled ?
20. What is the effect of the following if X = 20 and Y = 90?
     ```
     IF X >= 40 THEN
     IF Y > 50 THEN MOVE '*' TO Z
     ELSE MOVE '£' TO Z END-IF
     ELSE MOVE '%' TO Z END-IF.
     ```
     Set the code out so that it is easier to understand.

53.   Worked Project 1 - Stock Report

1. Produce a program which will allow a user to key in details of items in stock and which will save these details as a sequential file on disk - each record being in the form:

STOCK NUMBER	alphanumeric	5 characters
DESCRIPTION	alphanumeric	20 characters
QUANTITY IN STOCK	numeric	6 digits
REORDER LEVEL	numeric	6 digits
REORDER QUANTITY	numeric	6 digits
SUPPLIER NAME	alphanumeric	30 characters

2. Produce a program which will read the stock-file created above and display a report on the screen showing the stock number, description, quantity to reorder and supplier name for each item which needs to be reordered.

TACKLING THE PROJECT

For each program the following should be produced:
1.   a design - probably in the form of a structure diagram;
2.   a list of paragraph names to be used;
3.   a list of data names and descriptions;
4.   the program;
5.   a test plan;
6.   other documentation if appropriate.

PROGRAM 1

DESIGN

Overall, the program will have to open a file, carry out the main task of obtaining and saving data, then close the file - giving a structure diagram as follows:

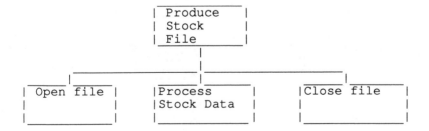

The main part of the program (dealing with all the stock data) will involve dealing with the first stock item, then the next, and so on (i.e. a repetition) until there are no more stock items to be entered.

So the structure diagram can be expanded - to show how the main task breaks down into an iteration.

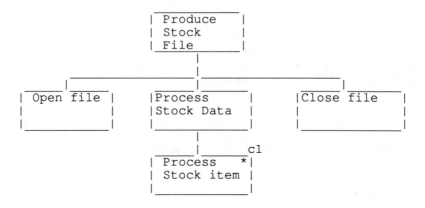

c1 - until no more stock items to be entered

Dealing with a single stock item will involve
1. displaying prompts inviting the users to key in the necessary details and accepting the data;
  and
2. storing it on disk.

It will also be necessary after each stock item to check whether there are any more stock items to be entered.

So the structure diagram can be expanded again to show how the task of Process Stock Item breaks down into a sequence of smaller tasks.

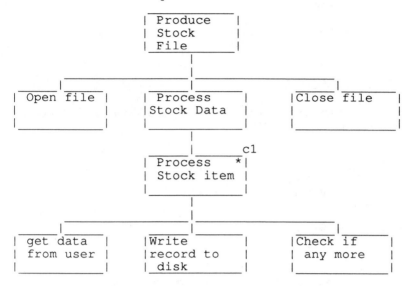

c1 - until no more stock items to be entered

PARAGRAPHS

The next stage is to make up paragraph names corresponding to the boxes in the completed diagram - e.g.
PRODUCE-STOCK-FILE-MAIN.
OPEN-STOCK-FILE.
PROCESS-STOCK-DATA.
CLOSE-STOCK-FILE.
PROCESS-STOCK-ITEM.
GET-DATA-FROM-USER.
WRITE-RECORD-TO-DISK.
CHECK-IF-ANY-MORE.

DATA ITEMS

Decide on a file name and suitable data names and write entries for the File Section of the Data Division.

```
FILE  SECTION.
FD    STOCK-FILE.
01    STOCK-RECORD.
      05    STOCK-NUMBER          PIC   X(5).
      05    STOCK-DESCRIPTION     PIC   X(20).
      05    STOCK-QUANTITY        PIC   9(6).
      05    REORDER-LEVEL         PIC   9(6).
      05    REORDER-QUANTITY      PIC   9(6).
      05    SUPPLIER-NAME         PIC   X(30).
```
Now decide on any additional fields that will be needed for working or other data.

A space will be needed to hold the user's answer to the question - 'Are there any more stock items to be entered'. This will only need to hold a 'Y' or 'N', so need only be one character - e.g.

```
WORKING-STORAGE SECTION.
01    ANY-MORE-STOCK-ITEMS      PIC  X.
```

THE PROGRAM CODE

Take the paragraphs you have already named - and fill them with COBOL code to make the PROCEDURE DIVISION.

```
PRODUCE-STOCK-FILE-MAIN.
     PERFORM OPEN-STOCK-FILE
     PERFORM PROCESS-STOCK-DATA
     PERFORM CLOSE-STOCK-FILE
     STOP RUN.

OPEN-STOCK-FILE.
     OPEN OUTPUT STOCK-FILE.

PROCESS-STOCK-DATA.
     PERFORM PROCESS-STOCK-ITEM UNTIL
       ANY-MORE-STOCK-ITEMS = 'N'.

CLOSE-STOCK-FILE.
     CLOSE STOCK-FILE.


PROCESS-STOCK-ITEM.
     PERFORM GET-DATA-FROM-USER
     PERFORM WRITE-RECORD-TO-DISK
     PERFORM CHECK-IF-ANY-MORE.

GET-DATA-FROM-USER.
     DISPLAY 'STOCK NUMBER ? (5 CHARACTERS)'
     ACCEPT STOCK-NUMBER

     DISPLAY 'DESCRIPTION OF STOCK ?'
     ACCEPT STOCK-DESCRIPTION

     DISPLAY 'QUANTITY IN STOCK (6 DIGITS) ?'
     ACCEPT STOCK-QUANTITY

     DISPLAY 'REORDER LEVEL (6 DIGITS)?'
     ACCEPT REORDER-LEVEL

     DISPLAY 'REORDER QUANTITY (6 DIGITS)?'
     ACCEPT REORDER-QUANTITY

     DISPLAY 'SUPPLIER NAME?'
     ACCEPT SUPPLIER-NAME.

WRITE-RECORD-TO-DISK.
     WRITE STOCK-RECORD.
```

```
CHECK-IF-ANY-MORE.
        DISPLAY 'ANY MORE STOCK ITEMS TO ENTER ?'
        ACCEPT ANY-MORE-STOCK-ITEMS.
```

Now write an *IDENTIFICATION DIVISION* and an *ENVIRONMENT DIVISION* and place them at the beginning of the program.

e.g.
```
IDENTIFICATION DIVISION.
PROGRAM-ID.   STOCK-PROGRAM-1.

ENVIRONMENT DIVISION.
INPUT-OUTPUT SECTION.
FILE-CONTROL.
SELECT STOCK-FILE ASSIGN TO 'STOCK'
ORGANIZATION IS SEQUENTIAL.
```

TEST PLAN

It is important to test the program - to ensure that it carries out the task of saving all the data that you key in.

As this program does not carry out any calculations or decisions - the testing is not difficult. Run the program and key in a small number of stock items - keeping a note of the details.

Use the appropriate facility of your operating system to look at the resulting file called 'STOCK'.

For example, if you are using a microcomputer and the MS-DOS operating system you would key in *TYPE STOCK* after running your program.

If you are using a UNIX system, key in *cat STOCK* in order to list the data file.

The file displayed should include all the data you keyed in while your program was running - note that it will be squashed together - exactly as it was written to disk.

Ensure that all the information has been written correctly and in the correct order.

PROGRAM 2

DESIGN

Once again, as the program handles a file of data - this time to read it and process the information - the task will involve opening the file, processing the data and then closing the file - giving a structure diagram top layer similar to that for program 1.

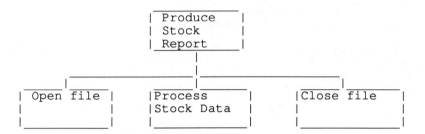

Processing the stock data will involve repetitively processing stock records - until the end of the file.

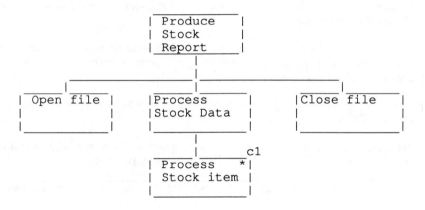

c1 - until end of file

Processing a stock item will involve reading the record from the disk file and deciding whether it needs to be reordered.

So the structure diagram will be expanded as follows:

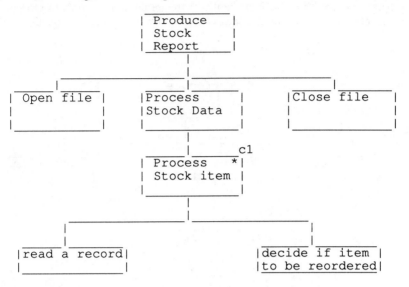

c1 - until end of file

With this sequence of events, the computer will in each case try to read a record and then decide if the item is to be reordered. This causes a problem after the last record is read, as the next attempt to read will simply get an end-of-file marker and the computer will generally leave the record details in memory unchanged from the previous one. This means that the decision to reorder the last stock-item will be taken twice.

The usual way to get around this problem is to read one record before starting the repetition of processing stock items. This means that the first task to be carried out within the repetition is that of deciding whether to reorder or not - followed by getting another record. If this read simply finds an end-of-file marker then the program can set a field to indicate that there are no more records to process and the repetition can finish on the basis of testing this field. (See Lesson 50).

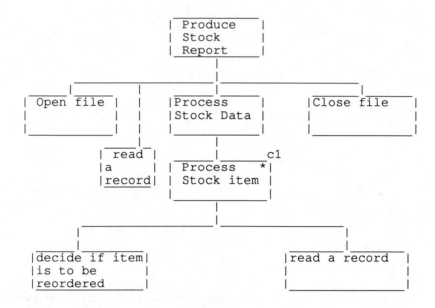

c1 - until end of file

78

Deciding whether the item needs to be reordered will consist of either displaying a report or doing nothing.

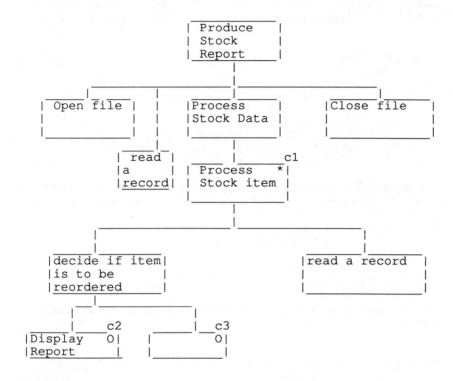

c1 - until end of file
c2 - if quantity in stock less than or equal to reorder level.
c3 - if quantity in stock greater than reorder level.

PARAGRAPHS

Create suitable paragraph names relating to the rectangles on the structure diagram - e.g.

PRODUCE-STOCK-REPORT-MAIN.
OPEN-STOCK-FILE.
PROCESS-STOCK-DATA.
CLOSE-STOCK-FILE.
PROCESS-STOCK-ITEM.
READ-A-RECORD
DECIDE-IF-REORDER.
DISPLAY-REPORT.

Note that the read a record rectangle appears twice on the structure diagram but only one copy of the paragraph is needed - as it can be PERFORMED from anywhere in the program.

79

DATA ITEMS

The File Section will look the same as the one in Program 1. As Program 2 has to read the file created by Program 1, the layout of the records and their length must be the same. The names could be changed if the programmer wanted to do so.

```
FILE SECTION.
FD   STOCK-FILE.
01   STOCK-RECORD.
        05   STOCK-NUMBER         PIC  X(5).
        05   STOCK-DESCRIPTION    PIC  X(20).
        05   STOCK-QUANTITY       PIC  9(6).
        05   REORDER-LEVEL        PIC  9(6).
        05   REORDER-QUANTITY     PIC  9(6).
        05   SUPPLIER-NAME        PIC  X(30).
```

The Working-Storage Section will need a space to store an indicator which can be set when the computer finds the end of the data file while reading records - e.g.

```
WORKING-STORAGE SECTION.
01   END-OF-FILE-INDICATOR PIC X.
```

THE PROGRAM CODE

Working downwards on the structure diagram - each paragraph can be coded as follows.

```
PRODUCE-STOCK-REPORT-MAIN.
     PERFORM OPEN-STOCK-FILE
     PERFORM READ-A-RECORD
     PERFORM PROCESS-STOCK-DATA
     PERFORM CLOSE-STOCK-FILE
     STOP RUN.
```

As usual, this main paragraph summarises the whole job.

```
OPEN-STOCK-FILE.
     OPEN INPUT STOCK-FILE.

PROCESS-STOCK-DATA.
     PERFORM PROCESS-STOCK-ITEM
     UNTIL END-OF-FILE-INDICATOR = 'E'.

CLOSE-STOCK-FILE.
     CLOSE STOCK-FILE.
```

Note that as the rectangle READ-A-RECORD appears twice in the structure diagram, it will need to be performed from two different places in the program - but it will only need to be coded once.

```
PROCESS-STOCK-ITEM.
     PERFORM DECIDE-IF-REORDER
     PERFORM READ-A-RECORD.
```

```
DECIDE-IF-REORDER.
    IF STOCK-QUANTITY <= REORDER-LEVEL
    THEN
        PERFORM DISPLAY-REPORT
    END-IF.
READ-A-RECORD.
    READ STOCK-FILE
        AT END MOVE 'E' TO END-OF-FILE-INDICATOR
    END-READ.
DISPLAY-REPORT.
    DISPLAY 'STOCK NUMBER ', STOCK-NUMBER
    DISPLAY 'STOCK DESCRIPTION', STOCK-DESCRIPTION
    DISPLAY 'QUANTITY TO REORDER ', REORDER-QUANTITY
    DISPLAY 'SUPPLIER NAME ', SUPPLIER-NAME.
```

TEST PLAN

This program is a little more complicated to test than the first one.

In particular, the program should be given data which will thoroughly test each condition on the structure diagram together with realistic data that might commonly be keyed in (base this on what your program is supposed to do from the original specification).

The conditions which need to be tested are:
1.   does the program end correctly ?
2.   does it display reports for all items which need to be reordered and only those items ?

In addition, the figures and information produced should be checked together with report's layout.

So decide on suitable test data and key it in to create a file - using Program 1. Then run Program 2 and check that the results are as expected.

Set the test data out in a manner which clearly shows what each data record is intended to check.
e.g.

1
STOCK-NUMBER	=	A2003
STOCK-DESCRIPTION	=	BAKED BEANS
STOCK-QUANTITY	=	050000
REORDER-LEVEL	=	020000
REORDER QUANTITY	=	010000
SUPPLIER NAME	=	A & B SUPPLIES

expected output - NO REPORT DISPLAYED

tests
Condition c3 (Quantity in stock greater than reorder level)

```
2
STOCK-NUMBER          =      A2004
STOCK-DESCRIPTION     =      SPAGHETTI
STOCK-QUANTITY        =      010000
REORDER-LEVEL         =      020000
REORDER QUANTITY      =      010000
SUPPLIER NAME         =      A & B SUPPLIES
```

expected output - REPORT DISPLAYED showing
STOCK NUMBER - A2004
STOCK DESCRIPTION - SPAGHETTI
QUUANITY TO REORDER - 010000
SUPPLIER NAME - A & B SUPPLIES

tests
Condition c2 (Quantity in stock less than reorder level)

```
3
STOCK-NUMBER          =      A2005
STOCK-DESCRIPTION     =      TOMATOES
STOCK-QUANTITY        =      010000
REORDER-LEVEL         =      010000
REORDER QUANTITY      =      010000
SUPPLIER NAME         =      X & Y SUPPLIES
```

expected output - REPORT DISPLAYED showing
STOCK NUMBER - A2005
STOCK DESCRIPTION - TOMATOES
QUANTITY TO REORDER - 010000
SUPPLIER NAME - A & B SUPPLIES

tests
Condition c2 (Quantity in stock equals reorder level)

A test log can then be made out showing the date and time of each run and whether the actual results coincided with the expected results. This could be shown against each record - or a separate sheet made out showing the result against each record number.

Keep printed copies of the program at each stage of development - ensure they are dated and timed so that you can easily see which is the most up-to-date version. Comment on each change and why it was made.

54. Suggested Programming Projects

For each of the following projects - produce structure diagrams, a list of paragraph names to be used, a written version of the program before testing, a test plan and log, comments on any changes that were necessary to cure logic errors and a printout of the final correct version of the program.

1.   An estate agent needs to be able to display (on the screen) a report on all properties under £100,000. Produce the following:

Program 1 - which will allow the user to key in details of properties and store them in a sequential file. Details should include:

address	alphanumeric	100 characters
number of rooms	numeric	2 digits
name of vendor	alphanumeric	20 characters
price	numeric	6 digits

Program 2 - which will read the file created by Program 1 and display a report showing details of all properties under £100,000.

2.   A school needs to be able to keep records of students marks and be able to produce a list of pupils who are to receive prizes. Produce the following:

Program 1 - which will allow the teacher to key in details about each student and store them on disk. Details should include:

name	alphanumeric	20 characters
Maths mark	numeric	3 digits
English mark	numeric	3 digits
Physics mark	numeric	3 digits
French mark	numeric	3 digits

Program 2 - which will read the file created by Program 1 and display a list of all students whose average mark is greater than 70 - with the overall heading 'Prizes to be awarded to: '

3.   A bank needs to produce a list of all customers accounts that are overdrawn. Produce the following:

Program 1 - which will allow the user to key in details about each customer's account and store the information on disk. Details should include:

account number	numeric	9 digits
name	alphanumeric	20 characters
address	alphanumeric	100 characters
account balance at beginning of day	numeric	9 digits including pence

(Remember that this item could be positive or negative)

credit item	numeric	6 digits including pence
debit item	numeric	6 digits including pence

Program 2 - which will read the file created by Program 1 and display a report showing all customers who are overdrawn by the end of the day - including the names, account numbers and amount overdrawn.

55.   Using FILLER and VALUE

FILLER can be used instead of a dataname if you wish to set aside an area of storage but do not need to be able to refer to it by name. It is often used when setting out lines of text (in memory) ready for display on the screen or for output to a printer.

Each FILLER that you use is usually given a VALUE (often spaces) to indicate the contents of that memory area (and therefore how it will appear on the print-out or screen).

```
e.g. 01   PRINT-HEADING.
          05   FILLER PIC X(5)   VALUE 'NAME'.
          05   FILLER PIC X(20)  VALUE SPACES.
          05   FILLER PIC X(4)   VALUE 'MARK'.
```
(Note that the word SPACES may be used to fill a data item with spaces).

When this item of data is DISPLAYed - the following will appear on the screen:

NAME   **MARK**

(Note the 20 spaces between the words).

Similarly a line of print may be set up with a mixture of variable data and fixed values.

```
e.g. 01   PRINT-LINE.
          05   STUDENT-NAME PIC X(20).
          05   FILLER       PIC X(5) VALUE SPACES.
          05   STUDENT-MARK PIC 999.
```

The name and mark can then be MOVEd from another area of store (possibly after READing them from a file) or ACCEPTed from the keyboard and then DISPLAYed in the form (e.g.):

JULIA   097

(Note how PRINT-LINE has been specified so that the items will line up under the headings in PRINT-HEADING).

The word FILLER itself may be omitted - e.g. 01 PIC X(5) VALUE SPACES.

Exercise
1.   Write a program which will request a student's name, course title and grade - then display the information in one line with suitable spacing between each field.
2.   Write a program which will display the heading:
     EMPLOYEE NAME   **WAGE**
     then read the file 'staff' (created by the program you wrote as an exercise in lesson 46) and display each employee's details as a line of text - e.g.
     WILLIAM SMITH   **100**
     ANNE JONES   **110**
     DAVID ANDREWS   **150**

56. Using a Printer

Output on the screen is suitable for many uses - but often a hard copy (i.e. printed on paper) will be required.
A document to be printed is treated as a file and each line is seen as a record. So if you want to use the printer - the Environment Division has to have an entry specifying a file name and the device (often just 'PRINTER') - e.g.
SELECT STUDENT-REPORT-FILE ASSIGN TO PRINTER.
(This will vary between computer systems - so consult the COBOL manual).

As with any other file, the File Section of the Data Division must have a suitable area specified to hold one record (line) until it is ready to be written. This line will be the same length as the line-length being used on your printer (e.g. 80 or 132 characters) - e.g.

```
FD STUDENT-REPORT-FILE
01 STUDENT-REPORT-LINE PIC X(80).
```

As each line on the report will have a different layout - it is normal to have a number of different working lines in the Working-Storage Section - but these will each be the same length as the report-line already specified - e.g.

```
01  STUDENT-NAME-LINE.
    05 FILLER PIC X(11) VALUE 'REPORT FOR '.
    05 STUDENT-NAME PIC X(30).
    05 FILLER PIC X(39) VALUE SPACES.
01  STUDENT-GRADE-LINE.
    05 FILLER PIC X(6) VALUE 'GRADE '.
    05 STUDENT-GRADE PIC X(15).
    05 FILLER PIC X(59) VALUE SPACES.
```

Within the Procedure Division, as with any other file, the printer file has to be opened and each line is written to the file when it is ready (generally after being moved from the relevant working-storage line).
e.g.

```
PRODUCE-STUDENT-REPORT-MAIN.
    PERFORM OPEN-REPORT-FILE
    PERFORM GET-STUDENT-DETAILS
    PERFORM PRINT-REPORT
    PERFORM CLOSE-REPORT-FILE
    STOP RUN.

OPEN-REPORT-FILE.
    OPEN STUDENT-REPORT-FILE.

GET-STUDENT-DETAILS.
    DISPLAY 'NAME ?' ACCEPT STUDENT-NAME
    DISPLAY 'GRADE ?' ACCEPT STUDENT-GRADE.

PRINT-REPORT.
    MOVE STUDENT-NAME-LINE TO STUDENT-REPORT-LINE
    WRITE STUDENT-REPORT-LINE
    MOVE STUDENT-GRADE-LINE TO STUDENT-REPORT-LINE
    WRITE STUDENT-REPORT-LINE.

CLOSE-REPORT-FILE.
    CLOSE STUDENT-REPORT-FILE.
```

57. Using Edited Fields

Data usually has to be presented in a well-set-out manner - and so that it can be easily understood. *Edited fields* help a great deal to achieve this.

For example, if a field containing a decimal point is to be used for calculations, it is quicker for the computer to note the position of the point without actually storing it as a separate character - so if a field has been defined as PIC 999V99 - then 125.25 would be stored as |1|2|5|2|5| and if this were printed out would appear as 12525 (somewhat misleading). To avoid this - the data is MOVEd into an edited field before it is displayed. In this example a suitable edited field might be defined as PIC 999.99.

It can be useful also to place commas between the thousands positions - e.g. 325,245.22.
This can be achieved by defining a field as PIC 999,999.99 - and once all the calculations have been done in a normal numeric field then the answer can be MOVEd into the edited field and printed out.

Sometimes additional characters are required to appear with a number - e.g. a pound or dollar sign. This is normally required to the immediate left of the number. A suitable edited field can be defined as PIC \$\$\$,\$\$9.99 - any numbers that need to occupy spaces containing dollar signs will simply overwrite them and a single dollar sign will appear to the left of the number. Sometimes asterisks are used on cheques to prevent numbers being added later - a suitable field could be defined as PIC \$**,***.99.

Likewise + or - signs are often required in an answer - immediately to the left of the number.
PIC ------.99 will give a - before a negative number but leave a positive number blank.
PIC ++++++.99 will put the appropriate sign before any number.

A numeric field will usually be displayed with leading zeroes (e.g. 00025), but these can be suppressed by moving the number into an edited field declared as PIC ZZZZ9 and displaying this.

Exercise
Write a program which will allow you to key in an employee's annual pay and which will then display a payslip showing the weekly pay in a suitable edited format. Try out various possible edited layouts.

58. *Using READ INTO and WRITE FROM*

Instead of using MOVE to copy a record from the Working-Storage Division into the File Section before writing it to disk - this can all be done with one command - e.g.

WRITE PRINT-LINE FROM HEADING-LINE
    AFTER ADVANCING 1 LINE.

(This assumes that PRINT-LINE is defined as a record in the FILE SECTION and that HEADING-LINE is the same length and is defined in the WORKING-STORAGE SECTION).

This can also be used for data-files on disk - not just Printer-files - e.g.

WRITE STUDENT-RECORD FROM FIRST-YEAR-STUDENT-DETAILS.

In a similar way if a record needs to be moved into an area of the Working-Storage Section after being read - then the command READ ... INTO may be used - which has the same effect as a READ followed by a MOVE - e.g.

READ STUDENT-FILE INTO FIRST-YEAR-STUDENT-DETAILS
    AT END MOVE 'E' TO END-OF-FILE-INDICATOR
END-READ.

Exercise
Write a program which will display the following text on a page:

```
A & B COMPUTING PLC
200 ELEPHANT STREET
LONDON E1

REPORT ON AX2000 COMPUTER
author - Anne Rogers
date   - 23/12/90
```

Make use of WRITE FROM.

59.   Multiple Record Types

Many files do not contain records of only one type - but might contain records of various formats and lengths.

For example, a file might consist mainly of ordinary student records of the following layout:

name	20 characters
address	60 characters
course code	5 characters

However, the student records might be grouped within the file according to the course the student is following - with a record at the end of each group giving information about the course with a layout as follows:

course code	5 characters
course name	20 characters
course tutor	20 characters
course description	40 characters.

It is possible to specify a number of different record types for one file as follows:

```
FD    STUDENT-FILE.
01    STUDENT-RECORD.
         05    STUDENT-NAME    PIC X(20).
         05    STUDENT-ADDRESS      PIC X(60).
         05    STUDENT-COURSE-CODE PIC X(5).
01    COURSE-RECORD.
         05    COURSE-CODE      PIC X(5).
         05    COURSE-NAME      PIC X(20).
         05    COURSE-TUTOR     PIC X(20).
         05    COURSE-DESCRIPTION   PIC X(40).
```

It is important to note that the two record descriptions are simply two ways of describing the *same* area of Central Memory.

Although the record lengths are the same in this case, this does not have to be so.

Note also that this method of redescribing an area of store can only be used at the 01 Level in the File Section. A different method is used in the Working-Storage Section.

Exercises
1.   Write a program which creates a file of student records (defined as above) interspersed with course records.
2.   Write a program which reads and displays the file.

60. Tests - Alphabetic/Alphabetic-upper/Alphabetic-lower

An item can be tested to check whether it is alphabetic (i.e. contains only letters of the alphabet or spaces):

e.g.(1)
```
IF STUDENT-NAME IS NOT ALPHABETIC
THEN
       DISPLAY 'ERROR'
END-IF.
```

e.g.(2)
```
IF STUDENT-GRADE IS ALPHABETIC
THEN
       PERFORM GRADE-ROUTINE
ELSE
       PERFORM ERROR-ROUTINE
END-IF.
```

A field can be validated as containing only upper-case (i.e. capital) letters or spaces:

e.g.
```
IF STAFF-NAME IS NOT ALPHABETIC-UPPER
THEN
       DISPLAY 'ERROR'
       MOVE '1' TO ERROR-FLAG
END-IF.
```

Similarly a field can be tested to check that it contains only lower-case letters or spaces:

e.g.
```
IF REPORT-COMMENT IS ALPHABETIC-LOWER
THEN
       PERFORM PRINT-REPORT
ELSE
       PERFORM ERROR-ROUTINE
END-IF.
```

Exercise
Write a program which will ask a prospective student for the following information: surname, first names, nationality - validating the data as it is keyed in.
Surname should be entered in capital letters, all other information can be entered in large or small letters.

61. Tests - Numeric/Positive/Negative/Zero

A field which is supposed to be numeric can be validated -
e.g.(1)
IF STUDENT-NUMBER IS NOT NUMERIC
THEN
    DISPLAY 'ERROR'
END-IF

e.g.(2)
IF ANNUAL-SALARY IS NUMERIC
THEN
    PERFORM CALCULATE-WEEKLY-PAY
ELSE
    PERFORM ERROR-ROUTINE.
END-IF.

A signed numeric field can be checked to see whether it is positive or negative -
e.g.(1)
IF ACCOUNT-BALANCE IS POSITIVE
THEN
    PERFORM CALCULATE-INTEREST
END-IF.

e.g.(2)
IF ACCOUNT-BALANCE IS NEGATIVE
THEN
    PERFORM PRINT-REMINDER
END-IF.

A number can also be tested to see if it is zero -
e.g.
IF STUDENT-MARK IS ZERO
THEN
    PERFORM WRITE-WARNING-LETTER
END-IF.

Exercise
1.   Write statements to check that valid data has been keyed into the following fields:
STAFF-NUMBER, ANNUAL-SALARY, DEPARTMENT-CODE (should be numeric), DATE (in form DDMMYY numeric).
2.   Write a statement which will tell the computer to carry out a paragraph called SEND-CATALOGUE if a customer's account is in credit; a paragraph called SEND-BILL if a customer's account is in the red and SEND-LEAFLET if the customer's account is zero.

62. *Using AND/OR/NOT*

Sometimes a number of conditions have to be true before a particular action is taken - this can be expressed using **AND**.
e.g.
IF EXAM-MARK-1 >= 50
    AND EXAM-MARK >= 50
THEN
    MOVE 'PASS' TO GRADE
END-IF.
(i.e. the student has to get 50 or more in both exams to pass).

Sometimes any one of a number of possible conditions has to be true for the action to be taken - this can be expressed using **OR**.
e.g
IF EXAM-MARK-1 >= 50 OR
    EXAM-MARK-2 >= 50
THEN
    MOVE 'PASS' TO GRADE
END-IF.
(i.e. the student has to get 50 or more in either one of the exams to pass).

Sometimes it is more complicated - perhaps a student takes two exams and can pass by getting 50 or more in both exams *or* by getting 80 or more in either one. This can be expressed using ANDs and ORs together:

IF (EXAM-MARK1 >= 50 AND EXAM-MARK2 >= 50)
    OR EXAM-MARK1 >= 80 OR EXAM-MARK2 >= 80
THEN
    MOVE 'PASS' TO GRADE
END-IF.

(If there are a number of conditions it is usually clearer to use brackets to show which ones should be evaluated first - otherwise the assumption will be that ANDs are carried out before ORs).

A compound condition involving a single data item may be abbreviated. For example, it is possible to write either of the following:

IF MARK > 50 AND MARK < 80	IF MARK > 50 AND < 80
THEN	THEN
MOVE 'PASS' TO GRADE	MOVE 'PASS' TO GRADE
END-IF.	END-IF.

Exercises
Express the following conditions:
1.   a student will pass if he/she gets 50 or more in all three examinations;
2.   a student will pass if he/she gets 50 or more in any *one* of three examinations;
3.   a student will pass if he/she gets 50 or more in both exam 1 and exam 2 *or* in exam 3 alone.
4.   a student will pass if he/she gets 50 or more in any two of three exams.

63. Expressing Conditions using Level 88

A neat way of expressing conditions is to define them in the Data Division. For example, suppose that a data item called FINISHED-INDICATOR will be set to 'Y' when the user has finished inputting data - it is possible to give a name to the condition of having finished by using Level 88 under the data definition for the item:

```
01 FINISHED-INDICATOR PIC X.
      88 FINISHED                   VALUE 'Y','y'
```

In the Procedure Division - the statement -
PERFORM PROCESS-DATA-RECORD UNTIL FINISHED
may then be used instead of saying
PERFORM PROCESS-DATA-RECORD UNTIL FINISHED-IND = 'y' OR 'Y'.

This can be particularly useful if there is a whole range of possible conditions - as each may be given a name - e.g.

```
01 STUDENT-GRADE       PIC 999.
      88 GRADE-IS-FAIL                VALUE 0 THRU 49.
      88 GRADE-IS-PASS                VALUE 50 THRU 64.
      88 GRADE-IS-MERIT               VALUE 65 THRU 84.
      88 GRADE-IS-DISTINCTION         VALUE 85 THRU 100.
```

These names may then be used in the Procedure Division -
e.g.
It is then possible to say:
IF GRADE-IS-FAIL THEN PERFORM FAIL-ROUTINE END-IF.
rather than:
IF STUDENT-GRADE < 50 THEN PERFORM FAIL-ROUTINE END-IF.

Note that the Data Definition entry is saying that there is one Data Item called STUDENT-GRADE which can take a number of different values - and these values can be referred to by a name so that the Procedure Division becomes easier to read.

Exercise
A data item called YEAR-OF-COURSE can take values from 1 to 3. Complete suitable Data Division entries so that the following Procedure Division entry becomes valid:
```
IF FIRST-YEAR-STUDENT
THEN
   PERFORM FIRST-YEAR-ENROLMENT-PROC
ELSE
   IF SECOND-YEAR-STUDENT
   THEN
      PERFORM SECOND-YEAR-ENROLMENT-PROC
   ELSE
      PERFORM THIRD-YEAR-ENROLMENT-PROC
   END-IF
END-IF.
```

64. *Revision Test*

1. What is the use of FILLER ? (55)
2. What is the use of VALUE ? (55)
3. If the following is moved into the record area and written to a printer file - what will be the appearance of the resulting line of print ? (56)
   ```
   01     HEADING-LINE.
       05    FILLER PIC X(20) VALUE SPACES.
       05    FILLER PIC X(17) VALUE 'A AND B COMPUTING'.
       05    FILLER PIC X(43) VALUE SPACES.
   ```
4. How would the following line appear if it were printed out ? (56)
   ```
   01 STUDENT-DETAIL-LINE.
       05    FILLER PIC X(5) VALUE SPACES.
       05    FILLER PIC X(8) VALUE 'SURNAME '.
       05    STUDENT-SURNAME PIC X(15).
       05    FILLER PIC X(12) VALUE 'FIRST NAMES '.
       05    STUDENT-FIRST-NAMES PIC X(30).
       05    FILLER PIC X(10) VALUE SPACEs.
   ```
5. A stock-report is divided into columns showing:
   stock number (5 digits), name of item (20 chars), quantity in stock (4 digits) and cost (PIC 9999.99).
   Set out a suitable Working-Storage Section entry for column-headings for the report. (56)
6. Write a suitable Environment Division entry for a print file for a stock report. (56)
7. Write a suitable entry for the File Section of the Data Division. (56)
8. If the number 1235 is moved into a field defined as PIC $$$,$$9.99 - how will the number appear if it is printed ? (57)
9. If the number 1235 is moved into a field defined as PIC $**,**9.99 - how will the number appear if it is printed ? Why is this format often used on printed cheques ? (57)
10. Define an edited field such that if the value 895.22 is moved to it - it will appear as $895.22 and 1096.00 will apear as $1096.00. (57)
11. Define an edited field such that the value 125 will appear as +125 and -125 will appear as -125. (57)
12. Define an edited field such that the value 30.90 will appear as 30.90 and the value -30.90 will appear as -30.90. (57)
13. Define a Working-Storage entry for a print line which will produce a line such as the following:
    Gross pay $300.00   Tax $100.00 Net pay $200.00
    (allowing for pay up to $9999.99) and with suitable spacing.
14. Define a Working-Storage entry for a print line which will produce a line such as the following: Please pay $*****1.50.
15. Explain the difference between the following:
    a)   IF X > Y AND (P < W OR S > R) (62)
          THEN PERFORM PARA-1 END-IF.
    b)   IF X > Y AND P < W OR S > R
          THEN PERFORM PARA-1 END-IF.
16. Explain the use of Level 88. Give 3 examples. (63)

93

65. Worked Project 2 - Student Reports

1. Produce a program which will allow a user to key in details of a group of students and will save these details as a sequential file on disk - each record being in the form:

STUDENT NUMBER	alphanumeric	5 characters
SURNAME	alphanumeric	20 characters
FIRST NAMES	alphanumeric	30 characters
MATHS MARK (%)	numeric	3 digits
ENGLISH MARK (%)	numeric	3 digits
FRENCH MARK (%)	numeric	3 digits

2. Produce a program which will read the student-file created above and print a report for each student in the form:

```
-----------------------------------------------------------------
REPORT FOR surname, first names

MARKS:
        MATHS    - maths mark
        ENGLISH  - english mark
        FRENCH   - french mark

        AVERAGE MARK - average mark for three subjects

OVERALL GRADE - grade
-----------------------------------------------------------------
```

Note - grade will be Distinction, Merit, Pass or Fail depending on whether the student's average mark is 85 or more, 65 or more, 50 or more or below 50 respectively.

Exercise
What has to be produced for each program ? Look back to Project 1 if necessary.

PROGRAM 1

DESIGN

Overall, the program will have to open a file, carry out the main task of obtaining and saving data then close the file - giving a structure diagram as follows:

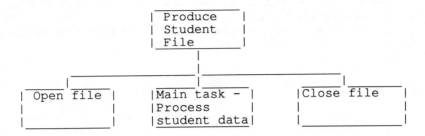

The main part of the program (dealing with all the student data) will involve dealing with the first student item, then the next, and so on (i.e. a repetition) until there are no more students to be entered.

So the structure diagram can be expanded - to show how the main task breaks down into an iteration.

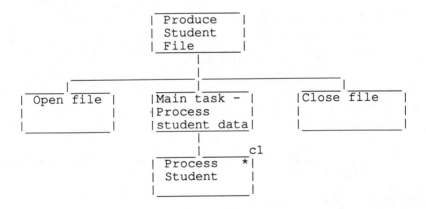

c1 - until no more students to be entered

Dealing with a single item will involve:

1.   displaying prompts inviting the users to key in the necessary details and
       accepting the data;
  and
2.   storing it on disk.

It will also be necessary after dealing with each student to check whether there are
any more students to be entered.
So the structure diagram can be expanded again to show how the task of Process
Student breaks down into a sequence of smaller tasks.

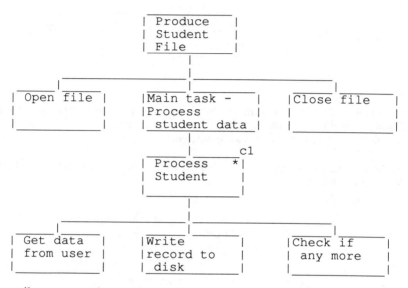

c1 - until no more students to be entered

PARAGRAPHS

The next stage is to make up paragraph names corresponding to the boxes in the
completed diagram - e.g.

PRODUCE-STUDENT-FILE-MAIN.
OPEN-STUDENT-FILE.
PROCESS-STUDENT-DATA.
CLOSE-STUDENT-FILE.
PROCESS-STUDENT.
GET-DATA-FROM-USER.
WRITE-RECORD-TO-DISK.
CHECK-IF-ANY-MORE.

DATA ITEMS

Decide on a file name and suitable data names and write entries for the File Section of the Data Division.

```
FILE SECTION.
FD    STUDENT-FILE.
01    STUDENT-RECORD.
      05    STUDENT-NUMBER         PIC  X(5).
      05    STUDENT-SURNAME        PIC  X(20).
      05    STUDENT-FIRST-NAMES    PIC  X(30).
      05    MATHS-MARK             PIC  9(3).
      05    ENGLISH-MARK           PIC  9(3).
      05    FRENCH-MARK            PIC  9(3).
```

Now decide on any additional fields that will be needed for working or other data. A space will be needed to hold the user's answer to the question - 'Are there any more student items to be entered'. This will only need to hold a Y or N so there need be only one character - e.g.

```
WORKING-STORAGE SECTION.
01   ANY-MORE-STUDENTS   PIC   X.
```

THE PROGRAM CODE

Take the paragraphs you have already named - and fill them with COBOL code to make the **PROCEDURE DIVISION**.

```
PRODUCE-STUDENT-FILE-MAIN.
      PERFORM OPEN-STUDENT-FILE
      PERFORM PROCESS-STUDENT-DATA
      PERFORM CLOSE-STUDENT-FILE
      STOP RUN.

OPEN-STUDENT-FILE
      OPEN OUTPUT STUDENT-FILE.


PROCESS-STUDENT-DATA.
      PERFORM PROCESS-STUDENT UNTIL
          ANY-MORE-STUDENTS = 'N' OR 'n'.

CLOSE-STUDENT-FILE.
      CLOSE STUDENT-FILE.


PROCESS-STUDENT.
      PERFORM GET-DATA-FROM-USER
      PERFORM WRITE-RECORD-TO-DISK
      PERFORM CHECK-IF-ANY-MORE.

GET-DATA-FROM-USER.
      DISPLAY 'STUDENT NUMBER ? (5 CHARACTERS)'
      ACCEPT STUDENT-NUMBER.
```

```
        DISPLAY 'STUDENT SURNAME?'
        ACCEPT STUDENT-SURNAME

        DISPLAY 'STUDENT FIRST NAMES?'
        ACCEPT STUDENT-FIRST-NAMES

        DISPLAY 'MATHS MARK ?'
        ACCEPT MATHS-MARK

        DISPLAY 'ENGLISH MARK ?'
        ACCEPT ENGLISH-MARK

        DISPLAY 'FRENCH MARK?'
        ACCEPT FRENCH-MARK.

WRITE-RECORD-TO-DISK.
        WRITE STUDENT-RECORD.

CHECK-IF-ANY-MORE.
        DISPLAY 'ANY MORE STUDENTS TO ENTER ?'
        ACCEPT ANY-MORE-STUDENTS.
```

Now write an *IDENTIFICATION DIVISION* and an *ENVIRONMENT DIVISION* and place them at the beginning of the program.
e.g.

```
IDENTIFICATION DIVISION.
PROGRAM-ID.  STUDENT-PROGRAM-1.

ENVIRONMENT DIVISION.
INPUT-OUTPUT SECTION.
FILE-CONTROL.
SELECT STUDENT-FILE ASSIGN TO 'STUDENTS'
ORGANIZATION IS SEQUENTIAL.
```

TEST PLAN

Run the program and key in a small number of students - keeping a note of the details.

Use the appropriate facility of your operating system to look at the resulting file called 'student'.

Check that the file displayed includes all the data you keyed in while your program was running and that all the information has been written correctly.

PROGRAM 2

DESIGN

Once again, as the program handles a file of data - this time to read it and process the information - the task will involve opening the file, processing the data and then closing the file - giving a structure diagram top layer similar to that for Program 1.

Note that as the information has to be printed out - a second file will be involved - this can be opened and closed at the same time as the student data file.

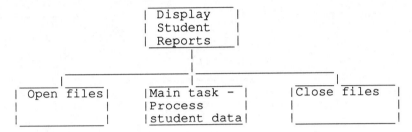

Processing the student data will involve repetitively processing student records - until the end of the file.

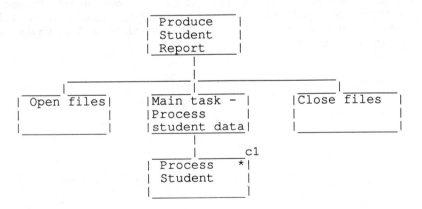

c1 - until end of file

Processing a student will involve reading the record from the disk file, calculating the average mark, deciding on the grade and printing a report.

So the structure diagram will be expanded as follows:

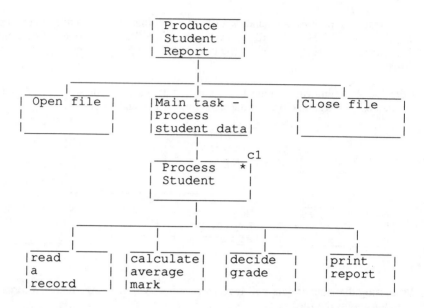

However as with the second program of Project 1 - it is better to attempt to read a record before starting the main processing - so that the computer always knows in advance whether the end of the file has been reached. So the structure diagram changes - as in Project 1.

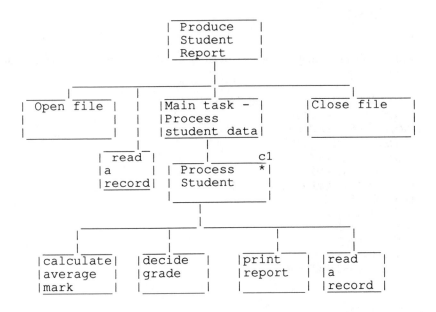

c1 - until end of file

Deciding the grade needs to be broken down further.

It involves making a selection - and so breaks down as shown:

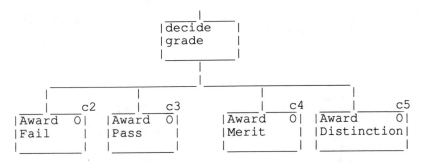

c2 - If average mark is less than 50
c3 - If average mark is 50 or more but less than 65
c4 - If average mark is 65 or more but less than 85
c5 - If average mark is 85 or more

PARAGRAPHS

Create suitable paragraph names relating to the rectangles on the structure diagram - e.g.

PRODUCE-STUDENT-REPORT-MAIN.
OPEN-STUDENT-FILE.
PROCESS-STUDENT-DATA.
CLOSE-STUDENT-FILE.
PROCESS-STUDENT.
READ-A-RECORD.
CALCULATE-AVERAGE-MARK.
DECIDE-GRADE.
PRINT-REPORT.
AWARD-FAIL.
AWARD-PASS
AWARD-MERIT.
AWARD-DISTINCTION.

DATA ITEMS

The File Section will contain two entries - one for the student data file and the other for the print file.

The first will look the same as the one in Program 1. As Program 2 has to read the file created by Program 1 - the layout of the records and their length must be the same.

The second will be a simple entry defining an area in central memory sufficient to hold one line of print (e.g. 80 or 132 characters).

```
FILE SECTION.

FD    STUDENT-FILE.
01    STUDENT-RECORD.
      05    STUDENT-NUMBER            PIC X(5).
      05    STUDENT-SURNAME           PIC X(20).
      05    STUDENT-FIRST-NAMES       PIC X(30).
      05    MATHS-MARK                PIC 9(3).
      05    ENGLISH-MARK              PIC 9(3).
      05    FRENCH-MARK               PIC 9(3).

FD    STUDENT-REPORT-FILE.
01    STUDENT-REPORT-LINE             PIC   X(80).
```

The Working-Storage Section will need a space to store an indicator which can be set when the computer finds the end of the student data file while reading records e.g.

```
WORKING-STORAGE SECTION.
01    END-OF-FILE-INDICATOR PIC X.
```

102

It will also contain a number of working spaces to build up lines of print before moving them to the space in the file section and writing them to the printer file.

e.g.

```
01    REPORT-LINE-1.
      05   FILLER PIC X(11) VALUE 'REPORT FOR '.
      05   REPORT-STUDENT-SURNAME  PIC  X(20).
      05   FILLER PIC X(2) VALUE ', '.
      05   REPORT-STUDENT-FIRST-NAMES PIC X(30).
      05   FILLER PIC X(17).

01    REPORT-LINE-2.
      05   FILLER PIC X(6) VALUE 'MARKS:'.
      05   FILLER PIC X(74) VALUE SPACES.

01    REPORT-LINE-3.
      05   FILLER PIC X(5) VALUE SPACES.
      05   FILLER PIC X(11) VALUE 'MATHS    - '.
      05   REPORT-MATHS-MARK PIC 9(3).
      05   FILLER PIC X(61) VALUE SPACES.

01    REPORT-LINE-4.
      05   FILLER PIC X(5) VALUE SPACES.
      05   FILLER PIC X(11) VALUE 'ENGLISH  - '.
      05   REPORT-ENGLISH-MARK PIC 9(3).
      05   FILLER PIC X(61) VALUE SPACES.

01    REPORT-LINE-5.
      05   FILLER PIC X(5) VALUE SPACES.
      05   FILLER PIC X(11) VALUE 'FRENCH   - '.
      05   REPORT-FRENCH-MARK PIC 9(3).
      05   FILLER PIC X(61) VALUE SPACES.

01    REPORT-LINE-6.
      05   FILLER PIC X(5)  VALUE SPACES.
      05   FILLER PIC X(15) VALUE 'AVERAGE MARK - '.
      05   REPORT-AVERAGE-MARK PIC 999.
      05   FILLER PIC X(57) VALUE SPACES.

01    REPORT-LINE-7.
      05   FILLER PIC X(16) VALUE 'OVERALL GRADE - '.
      05   OVERALL-GRADE PIC X(11).
      05   FILLER PIC X(53) VALUE SPACES.

01    REPORT-BORDER PIC X(80) VALUE ALL   '-'.
```

ALL indicates that all the 80 characters are to be filled with the value '-'.

THE PROGRAM CODE

Working downwards on the structure diagram - each paragraph can be coded as follows.

```
PRODUCE-STUDENT-REPORT-MAIN.
     PERFORM OPEN-FILES
     PERFORM READ-A-RECORD
     PERFORM PROCESS-STUDENT-DATA
     PERFORM CLOSE-FILES
     STOP RUN.
```

As usual, this main paragraph summarises the whole job.

```
OPEN-FILES.
     OPEN INPUT STUDENT-FILE
     OPEN OUTPUT STUDENT-REPORT-FILE.


PROCESS-STUDENT-DATA.
     PERFORM PROCESS-STUDENT
      UNTIL END-OF-FILE-INDICATOR = 'E'.

CLOSE-FILES.
     CLOSE STUDENT-FILE, STUDENT-REPORT-FILE.

PROCESS-STUDENT.
     PERFORM CALCULATE-AVERAGE-MARK
     PERFORM DECIDE-GRADE
     PERFORM PRINT-REPORT
     PERFORM READ-A-RECORD.

CALCULATE-AVERAGE-MARK.
     COMPUTE REPORT-AVERAGE-MARK =
     (MATHS-MARK + ENGLISH-MARK + FRENCH-MARK) / 3.

DECIDE-GRADE.
     EVALUATE TRUE
        WHEN REPORT-AVERAGE-MARK < 50
                         PERFORM AWARD-FAIL
        WHEN REPORT-AVERAGE-MARK >= 50 AND < 65
                         PERFORM AWARD-PASS
        WHEN REPORT-AVERAGE-MARK >= 65 AND < 85
                         PERFORM AWARD-MERIT
        WHEN REPORT-AVERAGE-MARK >= 85
                         PERFORM AWARD-DISTINCTION
     END-EVALUATE.
PRINT-REPORT.
     MOVE STUDENT-SURNAME TO REPORT-STUDENT-SURNAME
     MOVE STUDENT-FIRST-NAMES
         TO REPORT-STUDENT-FIRST-NAMES
     MOVE MATHS-MARK TO REPORT-MATHS-MARK
     MOVE ENGLISH-MARK TO REPORT-ENGLISH-MARK
     MOVE FRENCH-MARK TO REPORT-FRENCH-MARK
```

```
        MOVE REPORT-BORDER TO STUDENT-REPORT-LINE
        WRITE STUDENT-REPORT-LINE BEFORE ADVANCING 1
        MOVE REPORT-LINE-1 TO STUDENT-REPORT-LINE
        WRITE STUDENT-REPORT-LINE BEFORE ADVANCING 2
        MOVE REPORT-LINE-2 TO STUDENT-REPORT-LINE
        WRITE STUDENT-REPORT-LINE BEFORE ADVANCING 1
        MOVE REPORT-LINE-3 TO STUDENT-REPORT-LINE
        WRITE STUDENT-REPORT-LINE BEFORE ADVANCING 1
        MOVE REPORT-LINE-4 TO STUDENT-REPORT-LINE
        WRITE STUDENT-REPORT-LINE BEFORE ADVANCING 1
        MOVE REPORT-LINE-5 TO STUDENT-REPORT-LINE
        WRITE STUDENT-REPORT-LINE BEFORE ADVANCING 2
        MOVE REPORT-LINE-6 TO STUDENT-REPORT-LINE
        WRITE STUDENT-REPORT-LINE BEFORE ADVANCING 2
        MOVE REPORT-LINE-7 TO STUDENT-REPORT-LINE
        WRITE STUDENT-REPORT-LINE BEFORE ADVANCING 1
        MOVE REPORT-BORDER TO STUDENT-REPORT-LINE
        WRITE STUDENT-REPORT-LINE BEFORE ADVANCING PAGE.


AWARD-FAIL.
        MOVE 'FAIL' TO OVERALL-GRADE.
AWARD-PASS.
        MOVE 'PASS' TO OVERALL-GRADE.
AWARD-MERIT.
        MOVE 'MERIT' TO OVERALL-GRADE.
AWARD-DISTINCTION.
        MOVE 'DISTINCTION' TO OVERALL-GRADE.
```

Note that as the rectangle READ-A-RECORD appears twice in the structure diagram, it will need to be performed from two different places in the program - but it will need to be coded only once.

```
READ-A-RECORD.
        READ STUDENT-FILE
            AT END MOVE 'E' TO END-OF-FILE-INDICATOR
        END-READ.
```

TEST PLAN

Test the program by giving it data which will thoroughly check each condition on the structure diagram together with realistic data that might commonly be keyed in (base this on what your program is supposed to do from the original specification).

So the conditions which need to be tested are:

1.   does the program end correctly ?
2.   are the correct grades awarded ?

In addition the following points need to be checked:

1. are the calculations done correctly ?
2. are the reports set out correctly on the page ?

So decide on suitable test data and key it in to create a file - using Program 1.
Then run Program 2 and check that the results are as expected.

Note that when testing the award of grades, you should use at least three pieces of
test-data for each grade:
for example to check that a merit is awarded correctly, check what happens when
a student's average mark is - for example:
a)   64
b)   66
and
c)   65.

Set your test data out clearly to show what you are testing and what output you
expect.

For example:

Test record 1:
ANDREWS   JANE   MATHS MARK   =   040
                               ENGLISH MARK   =   060
                               FRENCH MARK   =   060

Expected Output:

```
REPORT FOR ANDREWS              , JANE

MARKS:
     MATHS    - 040
     ENGLISH  - 060
     FRENCH   - 060

     AVERAGE MARK - 53

OVERALL GRADE - PASS
```

---

66.   Worked Project 3 - Employee File Validation

1. Produce a program which will allow a user to key in details of employees and will save these details as a sequential file on disk - each record being in the form:

STAFF NUMBER	numeric	5 characters including check-digit (modulus 11)
SURNAME	alphanumeric	20 characters
FIRST NAMES	alphanumeric	30 characters
NATIONAL INSURANCE NUMBER	alphanumeric	9 characters
ADDRESS	alphanumeric	100 characters
DATE OF BIRTH	numeric	6 digits (ddmmyy)
ANNUAL SALARY	numeric	8 digits including 2 after decimal point

2. Produce a program which will read the staff-file created above and validate it - producing a printed report on any errors and a new staff-file containing all the records which have been checked to be valid.

Validation means checking that data is valid - i.e. possible for the type of data it is supposed to be. So if your program validates the surname - it might check that no numeric digits had been keyed in by mistake.

The checks that your program is required to make are as follows:

STAFF NUMBER	check-digit (modulus 11)
SURNAME	check all characters are alphabetic
FIRST NAMES	check all characters are alphabetic
NATIONAL INSURANCE NUMBER	should be two alphabetic characters followed by 6 numeric followed by 1 alphabetic.
ADDRESS	
DATE OF BIRTH	Year should be no later than '75 Month should be in the range 1 through 12 Day should be no greater than 31
ANNUAL SALARY	Largest salary = 200000

The error report for a record should show the contents of every field and flag those data items which are invalid as in 'error'.

PROGRAM 1

This is similar to Program 1 from each of the two previous projects.

PROGRAM 2

DESIGN

The program handles three files.

It reads the original staff-file created by Program 1, then writes a new staff-file containing only the records which have been checked as correct and a printer file containing a report on all the errors it has found.

So the structure diagram will be as follows:

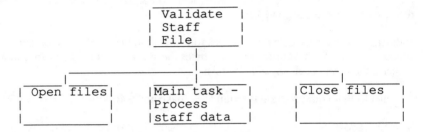

Processing the staff data will involve repetitively processing staff records - until the end of the file.

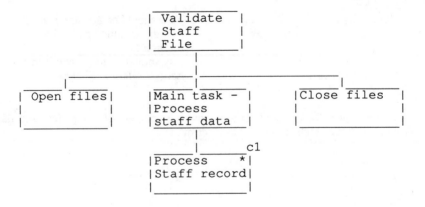

c1 - until end of file

108

Processing a staff record from the original file will involve reading the record from the disk file, checking each field and then deciding which new file to write the data to.

So the structure diagram will be expanded as follows:

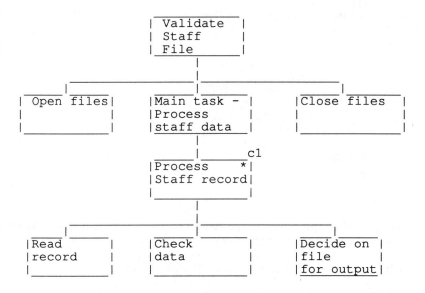

As usual it is better to read a record before starting the main processing.

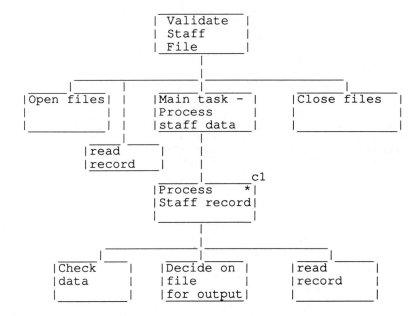

Checking data will involve checking each of the fields in turn - and some fields will require more than one check.

For example - the validation for the surname field will simply involve checking that only alphabetic characters have been entered and that the field has been filled (i.e. not just spaces).
So the structure diagram will be as follows:

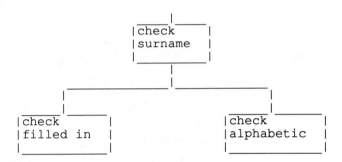

If either of these conditions is not met then an indicator field should be set to indicate whether or not the field is valid.

So this part of the structure diagram is expanded as follows:

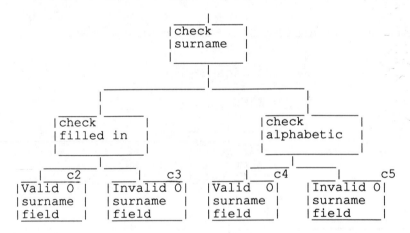

The check on the date of birth field is complicated and is best split into a number of parts:
1.   check that the field contains only numeric digits;
2.   check that the year is reasonable - given the likely age of employees;
3.   check that the month is 1 to 12;
4.   check that the day of the month is valid.

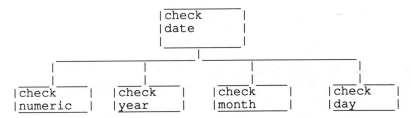

Each of these checks can be broken down into a selection.

The validation for the staff number field is also fairly complicated - it involves checking whether the field is numeric and then calculating whether the check-digit is correct.

A check-digit is an additional digit placed at the end of a number to help a computer to check whether the number has been correctly keyed. For example - suppose the correct staff number for a particular employee is 3591 and by mistake someone keys in 3519 - an easy mistake - it is useful if the computer is able to spot this. So before the number is issued to the employee an additional digit is calculated from the first 4 digits and placed at the end of the number - the most common method is called modulus 11 which means that it is based on the remainder after dividing by 11.

So, for the example each of the digits in the staff number is multiplied by a weight starting with 2 for the righthand digit, then 3 for the next and so on.

$$
\begin{array}{cccc}
3 & 5 & 9 & 1 \\
x5 & x4 & x3 & x2 \\
\hline
15 & 20 & 27 & 2
\end{array}
$$

The results are then added together and in this case come to 64.

This total is then divided by 11 and the remainder is noted (64/11 = 5 remainder 9). The remainder is then subtracted from 11 to give the check digit - in this case 2.

This check digit is then placed at the end of the number and the staff number becomes a 5 digit number - 35912.

You can then build it into your program to check the staff number by calculating that the check digit is correct - either by doing the calculation again and comparing to see if you get the same check digit or by the following method.

Multiply each of the digits in the staff number by a weight - starting with 1 for the rightmost digit:

$$
\begin{array}{ccccc}
3 & 5 & 9 & 1 & 2 \\
\underline{x5} & \underline{x4} & \underline{x3} & \underline{x2} & \underline{x1} \\
15 & 20 & 27 & 2 & 2
\end{array}
$$

Add these results together giving 66 and divide the total by 11. The remainder should be 0 - otherwise it means that the number has been keyed incorrectly.

Deciding which file to write to will involve writing either to the valid staff-file or to the error report file for printing, depending on whether any error indicator has been set.

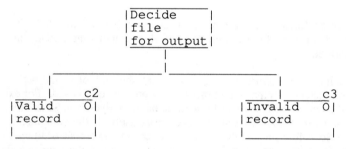

c2 - if error indicator = 0
c3 - if error indicator = 1

PARAGRAPHS

Create suitable paragraph names relating to the rectangles on the structure diagram - e.g.

VALIDATE-STAFF-FILE-MAIN.
OPEN-FILES.
PROCESS-STAFF-DATA.
CLOSE-FILES.
PROCESS-STAFF-RECORD.
READ-A-RECORD.
CHECK-DATA.
DECIDE-OUTPUT-FILE.
VALID-RECORD-PROCESS.
INVALID-RECORD-PROCESS.

The File Section entries for the old staff-file and the validated new staff-file will look the same as the one in Program 1. The entry for the error report file will be a record for the printer.

```
FILE SECTION.
FD STAFF-FILE.
01 STAFF-RECORD.
      05    STAFF-NUMBER.
            10 STAFF-NUMBER-DIGIT-1 PIC 9.
            10 STAFF-NUMBER-DIGIT-2 PIC 9.
            10 STAFF-NUMBER-DIGIT-3 PIC 9.
            10 STAFF-NUMBER-DIGIT-4 PIC 9.
            10 STAFF-NUMBER-DIGIT-5 PIC 9.
      05    SURNAME          PIC X(20)
      05    FIRST-NAMES      PIC X(30)
      05    N-I-NUMBER.
            10 N-I-NUM-CHARS-1-TO-2 PIC X(2).
            10 N-I-NUM-CHARS-3-TO-8 PIC X(6).
            10 N-I-NUM-CHARS-9      PIC X.

      05    STAFF-ADDRESS        PIC X(60).
      05    DATE-OF-BIRTH.
            10 DAY-OF-MONTH      PIC  99.
            10 MONTH            PIC  99.
            10 YEAR             PIC  99.
      05    ANNUAL-SALARY        PIC  9(6)V99.
```

Note that the date has been broken down into smaller fields to make it easier to check the individual parts.

```
FD VALID-STAFF-FILE.
01 VALID-STAFF-RECORD      PIC X(138).

FD ERROR-REPORT.
01 ERROR-LINE   PIC   X(80).
```

The Working-Storage Section will need a space to store an indicator which can be set when the computer finds the end of the data file while reading records - e.g.

```
WORKING-STORAGE SECTION.
01   END-OF-FILE-IND      PIC X.
```

Working spaces are needed to carry out the check-digit validation:

```
01   CHECK-TOTAL     PIC  9(7).
01   CHECK-RESULT    PIC  9(6).
01   CHECK-MOD       PIC  9(2).
```

Space will also be needed to hold lines that are being prepared for printing - how many will depend on how it is desired to present the error report - e.g. each field is to be presented on a separate line - then a line will be needed for each field with space for the data and an error indicator.

```
01    REPORT-LINE-1.
      05    REPORT-STAFF-NUMBER PIC 9(5).
      05    FILLER PIC X(5) VALUE SPACES.
      05    STAFF-NUMBER-ERROR-IND   PIC X(5).
      05    FILLER PIC X(65) VALUE SPACES.
01    REPORT-LINE-2.
      05    REPORT-SURNAME          PIC X(20).
      05    FILLER PIC X(5) VALUE SPACES.
      05    SURNAME-ERROR-IND    PIC X(5).
      05    FILLER PIC X(50) VALUE SPACES.
01    REPORT-LINE-3.
      05    REPORT-FIRST-NAMES PIC X(30).
      05    FILLER PIC X(5) VALUE SPACES.
      05    FIRST-NAMES-ERROR-IND    PIC X(5).
      05    FILLER PIC X(40) VALUE SPACES.
01    REPORT-LINE-4.
      05    REPORT-N-I-NUMBER    PIC X(9).
      05    FILLER PIC X(5) VALUE SPACES.
      05    N-I-NUMBER-ERROR-IND      PIC X(5).
      05    FILLER PIC X(61) VALUE SPACES.
01    REPORT-LINE-5.
      05    REPORT-ADDRESS          PIC X(60).
      05    FILLER PIC X(5) VALUE SPACES.
      05    ADDRESS-ERROR-IND    PIC X(5).
      05    FILLER PIC X(10) VALUE SPACES.
01    REPORT-LINE-6.
      05    REPORT-DATE-OF-BIRTH PIC 9(6).
      05    FILLER PIC X(5) VALUE SPACES.
      05    DATE-OF-BIRTH-ERROR-IND PIC X(5).
      05    FILLER PIC X(69) VALUE SPACES.
01    REPORT-LINE-7.
      05    REPORT-ANNUAL-SALARY      PIC 9(6)V99.
      05    FILLER PIC X(5) VALUE SPACES.
      05    ANNUAL-SALARY-ERROR-IND  PIC X(5).
      05    FILLER PIC X(69) VALUE SPACES.
01    REPORT-BORDER  PIC X(80) VALUE ALL '-'.
```

In addition a field which can be set when any error is found in a record will allow a speedy decision to be made whether to write the data to the valid staff file or the report file - e.g.

```
01  ERROR-IND  PIC 9.
```

It is important that this field and all the other error indicators in the report-lines are cleared before starting to process a new record - so a process of initialising the error indicators (i.e. setting them to zeroes or to spaces) should take place as part of processing a record - before the items are checked.

Exercise
Alter the structure diagram to take this into account.

THE PROGRAM CODE

Working downwards on the structure diagram - each paragraph can be coded as follows.

```
VALIDATE-STAFF-FILE-MAIN.
     PERFORM OPEN-FILES
     PERFORM READ-A-RECORD
     PERFORM PROCESS-STAFF-DATA
     PERFORM CLOSE-FILES
     STOP RUN.

OPEN-FILES.
     OPEN INPUT STAFF-FILE
     OPEN OUTPUT VALID-STAFF-FILE, ERROR-REPORT.

PROCESS-STAFF-DATA.
     PERFORM PROCESS-STAFF-RECORD UNTIL END-OF-FILE-IND
          = 'E'.

CLOSE-FILES.
     CLOSE STAFF-FILE, VALID-STAFF-FILE,
               ERROR-REPORT.

PROCESS-STAFF-RECORD.
     PERFORM INITIALISE-ERROR-FLAGS
     PERFORM CHECK-DATA
     PERFORM DECIDE-OUTPUT-FILE
     PERFORM READ-A-RECORD.

READ-A-RECORD.
     READ STAFF-FILE
          AT END MOVE 'E' TO END-OF-FILE-IND
     END-READ.

INITIALISE-ERROR-FLAGS.
     MOVE 0 TO ERROR-IND
     MOVE SPACES TO STAFF-NUMBER-ERROR-IND
                    SURNAME-ERROR-IND
                    FIRST-NAMES-ERROR-IND
                    ADDRESS-ERROR-IND
                    DATE-OF-BIRTH-ERROR-IND
                    N-I-NUMBER-ERROR-IND
                    ANNUAL-SALARY-ERROR-IND.

CHECK-DATA.
     PERFORM CHECK-STAFF-NUMBER
     PERFORM CHECK-SURNAME
     PERFORM CHECK-FIRST-NAMES
     PERFORM CHECK-ADDRESS
     PERFORM CHECK-DATE-OF-BIRTH
     PERFORM CHECK-N-I-NUMBER
     PERFORM CHECK-ANNUAL-SALARY.
```

```
DECIDE-OUTPUT-FILE.
     IF ERROR-IND = 0
     THEN
        PERFORM VALID-RECORD-PROCESS
     ELSE
        PERFORM INVALID-RECORD-PROCESS
     END-IF.

VALID-RECORD-PROCESS.
     MOVE STAFF-RECORD TO VALID-STAFF-RECORD
     WRITE VALID-STAFF-RECORD.
INVALID-RECORD-PROCESS.
     MOVE STAFF-NUMBER TO REPORT-STAFF-NUMBER
     MOVE SURNAME TO REPORT-SURNAME
     MOVE FIRST-NAMES TO REPORT-FIRST-NAMES
     MOVE STAFF-ADDRESS TO REPORT-ADDRESS
     MOVE DATE-OF-BIRTH TO REPORT-DATE-OF-BIRTH
     MOVE N-I-NUMBER TO REPORT-N-I-NUMBER
     MOVE ANNUAL-SALARY TO REPORT-ANNUAL-SALARY
     MOVE REPORT-BORDER TO ERROR-LINE
     WRITE ERROR-LINE BEFORE ADVANCING 2
     MOVE REPORT-LINE-1 TO ERROR-LINE
     WRITE ERROR-LINE BEFORE ADVANCING 1
     MOVE REPORT-LINE-2 TO ERROR-LINE
     WRITE ERROR-LINE BEFORE ADVANCING 1
     MOVE REPORT-LINE-3 TO ERROR-LINE
     WRITE ERROR-LINE BEFORE ADVANCING 1
     MOVE REPORT-LINE-4 TO ERROR-LINE
     WRITE ERROR-LINE BEFORE ADVANCING 1
     MOVE REPORT-LINE-5 TO ERROR-LINE
     WRITE ERROR-LINE BEFORE ADVANCING 1
     MOVE REPORT-LINE-6 TO ERROR-LINE
     WRITE ERROR-LINE BEFORE ADVANCING 1
     MOVE REPORT-LINE-7 TO ERROR-LINE
     WRITE ERROR-LINE BEFORE ADVANCING 2
     MOVE REPORT-BORDER TO ERROR-LINE
     WRITE ERROR-LINE BEFORE ADVANCING PAGE.

CHECK-STAFF-NUMBER.
     COMPUTE CHECK-TOTAL =
           (STAFF-NUMBER-DIGIT-1 * 5)
         + (STAFF-NUMBER-DIGIT-2 * 4)
         + (STAFF-NUMBER-DIGIT-3 * 3)
         + (STAFF-NUMBER-DIGIT-4 * 2)
         + (STAFF-NUMBER-DIGIT-5 * 1)
     DIVIDE CHECK-TOTAL BY 11 GIVING
         CHECK-RESULT REMAINDER CHECK-MOD
     IF CHECK-MOD NOT = 0
     THEN
         MOVE 1 TO ERROR-IND
         MOVE 'ERROR' TO STAFF-NUMBER-ERROR-IND
     END-IF.
CHECK-SURNAME.
     IF SURNAME IS NOT ALPHABETIC
     THEN
         MOVE 1 TO ERROR-IND
         MOVE 'ERROR' TO SURNAME-ERROR-IND
     END-IF.
```

```
CHECK-FIRST-NAMES.
     IF FIRST-NAMES IS NOT ALPHABETIC
     THEN
          MOVE 1 TO ERROR-IND
          MOVE 'ERROR' TO FIRST-NAMES-ERROR-IND
     END-IF.

CHECK-ADDRESS.
     EXIT.
CHECK-DATE-OF-BIRTH.
     IF YEAR > 75 MOVE 1 TO ERROR-IND
     THEN
          MOVE 'ERROR' TO DATE-OF-BIRTH-ERROR-IND
     ELSE
          IF MONTH > 12 OR < 1
          THEN
               MOVE 1 TO ERROR-IND
               MOVE 'ERROR' TO DATE-OF-BIRTH-ERROR-IND
          ELSE
               IF DAY-OF-MONTH  > 31 OR < 1
               THEN
                    MOVE 1 TO ERROR-IND
                    MOVE 'ERROR' TO
                         DATE-OF-BIRTH-ERROR-IND
               END-IF
          END-IF
     END-IF.
CHECK-ANNUAL-SALARY.
     IF ANNUAL-SALARY > 200000
          MOVE 1 TO ERROR-IND
          MOVE 'ERROR' TO ANNUAL-SALARY-ERROR-IND
     END-IF.
CHECK-N-I-NUMBER.
     IF N-I-NUM-CHARS-1-TO-2 IS NOT ALPHABETIC
     THEN
          MOVE 1 TO ERROR-IND
          MOVE 'ERROR' TO N-I-NUMBER-ERROR-IND
     ELSE
          IF N-I-NUM-CHARS-3-TO-8 IS NOT NUMERIC
          THEN
               MOVE 1 TO ERROR-IND
               MOVE 'ERROR' TO N-I-NUMBER-ERROR-IND
               IF N-I-NUM-CHARS-9 IS NOT ALPHABETIC
               THEN
                    MOVE 1 TO ERROR-IND
                    MOVE 'ERROR' TO
                         N-I-NUMBER-ERROR-IND
               END-IF
          END-IF
     END-IF.
```

TEST PLAN

The conditions which need to be tested are:

1. does the program end correctly ?
2. does it display reports for all those records which contain errors and only those records ?
3. are all valid records (and only valid records) written correctly to the valid staff file ?
4. is every different type of error dealt with correctly - i.e. does the word 'error' appear in the right place ?

So decide on suitable test data and key it in to create a file - using program 1.
Then run program 2 and check that the results are as expected.

67. Worked Project 4 - Control Break

Printed reports where sub-totals appear every so often are frequently required. This process is known as a 'Control Break' - the main flow of producing ordinary lines of print is broken off to produce a different type of print-line.

A department-store wishes to use a computer to produce sales figures each day.

Program 1

Produce a program which will allow data on sales to be entered as follows:

Department Number	numeric	3 digits
Stock code for item	alphanumeric	6 characters
Description of item	alphanumeric	20 characters
Number of items sold	numeric	6 digits
Price	numeric	6 digits including two decimal places

The program should save the information as a sequential file on disk.

Program 2

Produce a program which will read the file produced by Program 1 and produce a printed report with suitable headings at the top of each page and showing for each item: stock code, description, value of goods sold.

The total value of goods for each department should be totalled and printed at the bottom of the list for that department. The report, at the end, should include totals for the whole store.

Example Layout

```
Item Code        Description      Sales (£)

Department 001
X03120           WINE GLASS       520.50
X12304           DECANTER         200.00
Y09089           TEA SET          300.00
Z09023           TEA SET          500.00
X09087           DINNER SET      1000.00

TOTAL FOR DEPARTMENT 001 =       2000.50

Department 002
AC0002           SUIT             300.00
AC3000           SUIT             500.00
AC9087           SHIRT            400.00
AC9989           TIE              256.00

TOTAL FOR DEPARTMENT 002 =       1456.00
```

The program can assume that the file is in correct sequence (sorted on department code) - remember this when entering the data to test the program !

Exercise
Design and write Program 1

TACKLING PROGRAM 2

The program involves reading a file and producing another file (for the printer) -
so as usual the program at first breaks down into opening the files, producing a
report from the data and then closing the files.

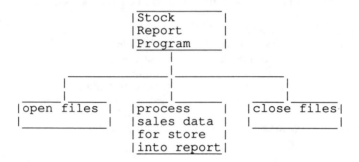

Processing the sales data into a sales report consists of writing headings for the
first page, processing all the data in the files into the main body of the report and
finally printing totals for the store.

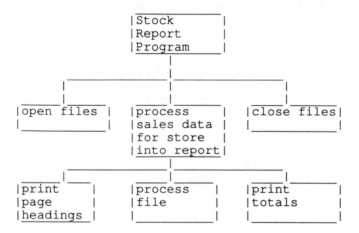

There are two main problems involved in processing the files:

1.	dealing with page breaks;
2.	dealing with control breaks.

The easiest way to look at the program is to deal with one of the problems first. The control breaks are an integral part of the report - so we shall look at these first.

One way of looking at the control breaks is to say that the process of dealing with the data-file breaks down into dealing with the data for the first department then for the next and so on - i.e. a repetition of dealing with a department.

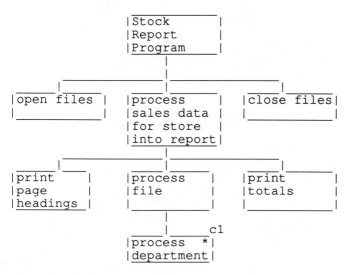

c1 - until end of file

For each department there will usually be a number of records - each one relating to a particular type stock item; so processing a department consists of writing a sub-heading, processing all the records for the department then doing the totals for the department.

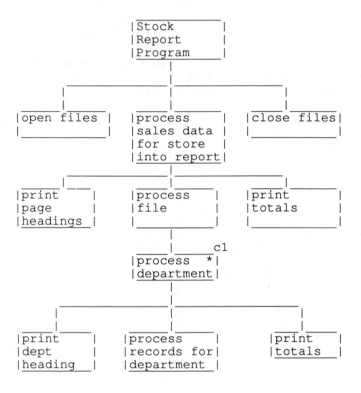

c1 - until end of file

Processing the records for a department consists of repeatedly processing individual records.

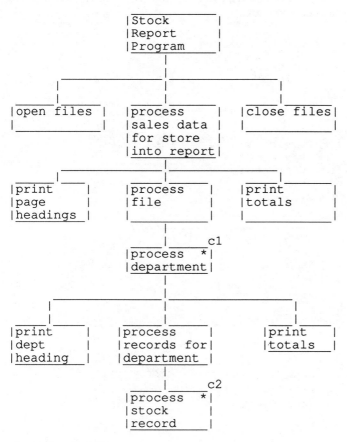

c1 - until end of file
c2 - until end of department

Processing a Stock Record will consist of reading a record, calculating the total value of goods sold and printing a line showing the information.

However, it is usual to read one record in advance at the very beginning of the program - which means that this data can be processed (i.e. calculations and printing and then another record read).

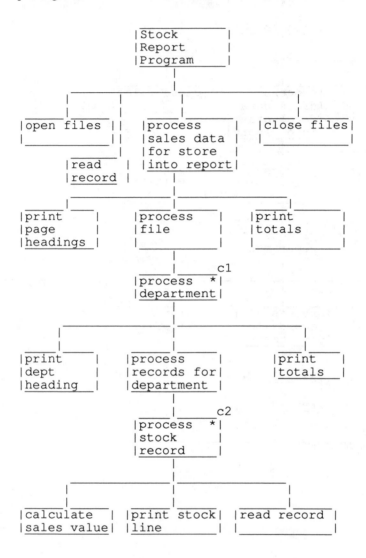

c1 - until end of file
c2 - until end of department

Printing involves the problem of checking when the printout reaches the end of the page. Suppose it is decided that there should be 20 lines to a page - then the program should add 1 to a count every time a line is printed (whether the line is a heading, a normal stock line, a sub-total, total, or extra blank line).

Printing will generally break down into moving the data into the Central Memory area reserved in the File Section for the printer file, writing the line and adding 1 to the count (or more if extra spacing is included such as around sub-totals or headings).

A standard paragraph can be written to take care of the actual write operation - this can decide whether a new page is necessary. This could be called from anywhere in the program but the calling paragraph would have to pass across the number of lines that are to be left before the write (this would be added to the line count). This means that the main part of the program can simply state that a line needs to be written and how much space is to be left and simply leave it to the Write-to-printer paragraph to decide whether a new page is needed.

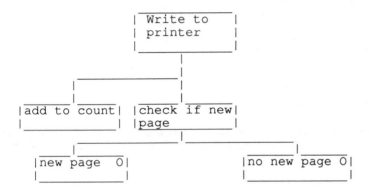

PARAGRAPHS

STOCK-REPORT-MAIN.
OPEN-FILES.
PROCESS-DATA-INTO-REPORT.
CLOSE-FILES.

READ-RECORD.

PRINT-PAGE-HEADING.
PROCESS-FILE.
PRINT-TOTALS.

PROCESS-DEPT.

PRINT-DEPT-HEADING.
PROCESS-RECORDS-FOR-DEPT.
PRINT-DEPT-TOTALS.

PROCESS-STOCK-RECORD.

CALC-SALES-VALUE.
PRINT-STOCK-LINE.

WRITE-TO-PRINTER.
ADD-TO-COUNT.
CHECK-IF-NEW-PAGE.
NEW-PAGE.
NO-NEW-PAGE.

DATA ITEMS

The File Section will need definitions for the two files:

```
FD    STOCK-FILE.
01    STOCK-RECORD.
      05    DEPT-NUMBER          PIC 999.
      05    STOCK-CODE           PIC X(6).
      05    STOCK-DESCRIPTION    PIC X(20).
      05    NUMBER-SOLD          PIC 9(6).
      05    PRICE                PIC 9(4)V99.

FD    STOCK-REPORT.
01    REPORT-LINE           PIC   X(80).
```

A number of different print layouts will be needed in the Working-Storage Section so that the data can be built up before transferring to the STOCK-RECORD and writing the record.

```
01    PAGE-HEADING.
      05 FILLER PIC X(10 ) VALUE 'Item code '.
      05 FILLER PIC X(11)  VALUE 'Description'.
      05 FILLER PIC X(19)  VALUE SPACES.
      05 FILLER PIC X(9)   VALUE 'Sales (£)'.
      05 FILLER PIC X(31)  VALUE SPACES.

01    DEPARTMENT-HEADING.
      05 FILLER PIC X(11)    VALUE 'Department '.
      05 HEADING-DEPT-NUMBER PIC 999.
      05 FILLER PIC X(66) VALUE SPACES.

01    DEPARTMENT-TOTALS.
      05 FILLER PIC X(10) VALUE 'TOTAL FOR '.
      05 FILLER PIC X(11) VALUE 'DEPARTMENT '.
      05 TOTALS-DEPT-NUMBER PIC 999.
      05 FILLER PIC X(16) VALUE SPACES.
      05 PRINT-DEPT-TOTAL PIC 9(6).99.
      05 FILLER PIC X(31) VALUE SPACES.

01    FINAL-TOTALS.
      05 FILLER PIC X(10) VALUE 'TOTAL FOR '.
      05 FILLER PIC X(6)  VALUE 'STORE'.
      05 PRINT-STORE-TOTAL PIC 9(7).99.
```

```
          05 FILLER PIC X(55) VALUE SPACES.

01    STOCK-ITEM-LINE.
          05 STOCK-CODE-PRINT PIC   999.
          05 FILLER PIC X(7) VALUE SPACES.
          05 STOCK-DESCRIPTION-PRINT PIC X(20).
          05 FILLER PIC X(10) VALUE SPACES.
          05 PRINT-SALES-VALUE PIC 9(6).99.
          05 FILLER PIC X(32).
```

In addition - as is usual with a program which reads files - an end-of-file indicator is needed.

```
01 END-OF-FILE-IND PIC X VALUE SPACE.
```

An area will be needed to keep track of the most recently processed department code so that it can be compared with the department code for the next record when it is read to see if the department has changed (for the Control Break).

```
01 CURRENT-DEPT-NUMBER PIC 999.
```

Also data items will be needed to keep track of how many lines have been printed on the page, how many are allowed and what spacing is required:

```
01    LINE-COUNT          PIC 99 VALUE 0.
01    LINES-PER-PAGE      PIC 99 VALUE 20.
01    LINE-SPACING        PIC 9.
```

The first two have been initialised to zero but this could be done later with a MOVE command if preferred.

Working space will be needed for calculations:

```
01    SALES-VALUE    PIC   9(6)V99.
01    DEPT-TOTAL     PIC   9(6)V99.
01    STORE-TOTAL    PIC   9(7)V99.
```

A temporary storage space will be needed to hold the current line while page headings are printed at a change of page:

```
01    TEMP-LINE      PIC X(80).
```

THE PROGRAM CODE

```
STOCK-REPORT-MAIN.
          PERFORM OPEN-FILES
          PERFORM READ-RECORD
          PERFORM PROCESS-DATA-INTO-REPORT
          PERFORM CLOSE-FILES
          STOP RUN.
```

```
OPEN-FILES.
    OPEN INPUT STOCK-FILE
    OPEN OUTPUT STOCK-REPORT.

PROCESS-DATA-INTO-REPORT.
    PERFORM PRINT-PAGE-HEADING
    PERFORM PROCESS-FILE
    PERFORM PRINT-TOTALS.

CLOSE-FILES.
    CLOSE STOCK-FILE, STOCK-REPORT.

READ-RECORD.
    READ STOCK-FILE
     AT END MOVE 'E' TO END-OF-FILE-IND
    END-READ.

PRINT-PAGE-HEADING.
    MOVE PAGE-HEADING TO REPORT-LINE
    MOVE 2 TO LINE-SPACING
    PERFORM WRITE-TO-PRINTER.

PROCESS-FILE.
    PERFORM PROCESS-DEPT UNTIL
        END-OF-FILE-IND = 'E'.

PRINT-TOTALS.
    MOVE STORE-TOTAL TO PRINT-STORE-TOTAL
    MOVE FINAL-TOTALS TO REPORT-LINE
    MOVE 4 TO LINE-SPACING
    PERFORM WRITE-TO-PRINTER.

PROCESS-DEPT.
    MOVE DEPT-NUMBER TO CURRENT-DEPT-NUMBER
    PERFORM PRINT-DEPT-HEADING
    PERFORM PROCESS-RECORDS-FOR-DEPT
    PERFORM PRINT-DEPT-TOTALS
    ADD DEPT-TOTAL TO STORE-TOTAL
    MOVE ZERO TO DEPT-TOTAL.

PRINT-DEPT-HEADING.
    MOVE CURRENT-DEPT-NUMBER TO HEADING-DEPT-NUMBER
    MOVE DEPARTMENT-HEADING TO REPORT-LINE
    MOVE 2 TO LINE-SPACING
    PERFORM WRITE-TO-PRINTER.

PROCESS-RECORDS-FOR-DEPT.
    PERFORM PROCESS-STOCK-RECORD
      UNTIL DEPT-NUMBER NOT = CURRENT-DEPT-NUMBER
      OR END-OF-FILE-IND = 'E'.

PRINT-DEPT-TOTALS.
    MOVE CURRENT-DEPT-NUMBER
        TO TOTALS-DEPT-NUMBER
    MOVE DEPT-TOTAL TO PRINT-DEPT-TOTAL
    MOVE DEPARTMENT-TOTALS TO REPORT-LINE
    MOVE 2 TO LINE-SPACING
    PERFORM WRITE-TO-PRINTER.
```

```
PROCESS-STOCK-RECORD.
     MOVE STOCK-CODE TO STOCK-CODE-PRINT
     MOVE STOCK-DESCRIPTION TO STOCK-DESCRIPTION-PRINT
     PERFORM CALC-SALES-VALUE
     MOVE SALES-VALUE TO PRINT-SALES-VALUE
     ADD SALES-VALUE TO DEPT-TOTAL
     PERFORM PRINT-STOCK-LINE
     PERFORM READ-RECORD.
CALC-SALES-VALUE.
     MULTIPLY NUMBER-SOLD BY PRICE
          GIVING SALES-VALUE.
PRINT-STOCK-LINE.
     MOVE STOCK-ITEM-LINE TO REPORT-LINE
     MOVE 1 TO LINE-SPACING
     PERFORM WRITE-TO-PRINTER.

WRITE-TO-PRINTER.
     PERFORM ADD-TO-COUNT
     PERFORM CHECK-IF-NEW-PAGE.
ADD-TO-COUNT.
     ADD LINE-SPACING TO LINE-COUNT.
CHECK-IF-NEW-PAGE.
     IF LINE-COUNT > LINES-PER-PAGE
     THEN
      PERFORM NEW-PAGE
     ELSE
      PERFORM NO-NEW-PAGE
     END-IF.
NEW-PAGE.
     MOVE REPORT-LINE TO TEMP-LINE
     MOVE PAGE-HEADING TO REPORT-LINE
     WRITE REPORT-LINE AFTER ADVANCING PAGE
     MOVE TEMP-LINE TO REPORT-LINE
     WRITE REPORT-LINE AFTER ADVANCING 2 LINES
     MOVE 3 TO LINE-COUNT.
NO-NEW-PAGE.
     WRITE REPORT-LINE AFTER ADVANCING LINE-SPACING.
```

TESTING

Use Program 1 to key in test data - ensure that the data is in order of department and all the stock-items for each department are grouped together.

Each condition needs to be tested - together with a realistic set of test data that would ensure the program would work under normal conditions.

Check that all calculations - sales figure, sub-totals and totals - are carried out correctly.

Check that control-breaks occur at the right place.

Check that paging takes place correctly.

68. Suggested Programming Project

For each of the following programs - produce structure diagrams, a list of paragraph names to be used, a written version of the program before testing, a test plan and log, comments on any changes that were necessary to cure logic errors and a printout of the final correct version of the program.

A college needs to store details of students' exam results on disk and produce a report showing passes and fails. Produce the following.

Program 1 - which allows the user to key in a record for each subject passed as follows:

subject code	4 digits (including modulus 11 check-digit)
subject name	20 characters
student surname	15 characters
student initials	2 characters
student course code	6 character (1 alphabetic + 5 numeric)
result	1 character (P or F)

When you run the program, type the information in so that it is in order of subject code and within this in alphabetical order of student name.

Program 2 - which will read the file produced by Program 1 and validate the following fields:

subject code
student course code
result

This program should produce a file containing all the valid records and a printed report showing each record that contains an error (separate page for each record) with an indication of which fields are invalid.

Program 3 - which will read the valid file produced by Program 2 and produce a report set out as follows:

```
Subject 0001    ENGLISH LANGUAGE
surname         initials course      result
ANDERSON        A        001245      PASS
JONES           WA       023000      FAIL
PATEL           PP       002345      PASS
*****************************************************
Subject 0001 - Total passes = 2, Total Fails = 1
*****************************************************
```

There should be a fresh page for each subject and in addition every 30 lines.
At the end of the report (on a fresh page) there should be totals for the number who took the exam, the number who passed and the number who failed.

69. *Sorting*

It is often necessary to sort the records in a file into order. The SORT command allows this to be done easily.

Generally, your program would specify:

1. the name of a work-file which the sort-routine can use;
2. the key-field on which the file will be sorted;
3. the name of the file which has to be sorted;
and
4. the name for the new sorted file.

e.g.

```
SORT WORK-FILE
    ASCENDING KEY STAFF-NUMBER
        USING UNSORTED-STAFF-FILE
            GIVING SORTED-STAFF-FILE.
```

Each of these should be defined in the Data Division's File Section in the normal way - but the first of these files (the work-file) should have an SD entry rather than an FD.
Note that the work-file records should be set out in the same way as the file which has to be sorted and the Sort key is specified as one of the fields in the work-file.
e.g.

```
SD    WORK-FILE.
01    STAFF-RECORD.
      05 STAFF-NUMBER     PIC 9(8).
      05 STAFF-NAME       PIC X(35).
      05 STAFF-ADDRESS    PIC X(60).
      05 STAFF-SALARY     PIC 9(5)V99.
FD    UNSORTED-STAFF-FILE.
01    UNSORTED-STAFF-RECORD    PIC X(110).

FD    SORTED-STAFF-FILE.
01    SORTED-STAFF-RECORD      PIC X(110).
```

The details of the records for the unsorted file and the new sorted file do not have to be specified for the sort routine as they are assumed to be the same as those of the work-file - you can of course spell out the details if you need them for another part of your program.

Note that you should not open files for the sort routine as it opens files itself automatically and closes them when it has finished.

Exercise
Write a program which will sort a file of student details into surname order.

70.   Using PERFORM .. VARYING

While carrying out a repetitive task, it is often useful to be able to keep count of how many times it is carried out.   This can be done using PERFORM .. VARYING.

Example

```
. . .
DATA DIVISION.
WORKING-STORAGE SECTION.
01    STUDENT-NUMBER PIC 99.

PROCEDURE DIVISION.
MAIN-PARA.
     PERFORM DISPLAY-STUDENT-NUMBER
        VARYING STUDENT-NUMBER FROM 1 BY 1
           UNTIL STUDENT-NUMBER > 10
     STOP RUN.

DISPLAY-STUDENT-NUMBER.
        DISPLAY 'HELLO'.
        DISPLAY STUDENT-NUMBER.
```

Ensure that the data item which will contain the count is big enough to hold the largest number in the sequence.

Note that you can alter the starting point for the count and the jumps in the count by altering the FROM and BY values - e.g.

PERFORM DISPLAY-STUDENT-NUMBER
 VARYING STUDENT-NUMBER FROM 10 BY 5
        UNTIL STUDENT-NUMBER >50.

This would start the student-number off at 10 and increase it to 15, then to 20 and so on until after it had reached 50.

Exercises
1.   Write a program which will display all the whole numbers from 1 to 100.
2.   Write a program which will display the numbers between 20 and 50 in intervals of 2.

71. Using Tables (Arrays) - Single Dimensional

If a number of similar items of data (e.g. the names of ten employees) have to be stored in Central Memory at the same time - these would usually be stored in a Table (also called an Array).

In the Data Division, memory-space would be set aside for such a table as follows:

e.g.   01   EMPLOYEE-TABLE.
            05   EMPLOYEE-NAME PIC X(20) OCCURS 10.
Reserves space for employee-table which consists of 10 employee-names (i.e. occurs 10) - each 20 characters long.

In the Procedure Division, if you want - for example - to display one particular item in the table - it would be referred to by the dataname followed by a number in brackets:

e.g.   DISPLAY EMPLOYEE-NAME(3)
would cause the third name in the table to be displayed on the screen.

Alternatively, instead of placing an actual number in the brackets - the required value may be placed in a suitable numeric data item, which may then be quoted in the brackets:

e.g.   MOVE 3 TO EMP-NO.
            DISPLAY EMPLOYEE-NAME(EMP-NO).

The following piece of code would allow the table to be filled - one item at a time - with data typed in from the keyboard:

```
PERFORM VARYING EMP-NO FROM 1 BY 1 UNTIL EMP-NO > 10
        DISPLAY 'KEY IN A NAME'
        ACCEPT EMPLOYEE-NAME(EMP-NO).
END-PERFORM.
```

(Note EMP-NO would be declared as PIC 99 - it is important that the number of digits allowed for this data item is sufficient to allow all the items in the table to be accessed).

Exercises
1.   How much space is occupied by EMPLOYEE-TABLE (above)?
2.   What happens to a table of data when the program finishes running ?
3.   Write a Data Division entry for a table to hold the names of 10 students - each 30 characters long.
        How much space is occupied by the table ?
4.   Write a program to accept the 10 names, one-by-one and store them in memory; then display them all in a list.
5.   Alter the program from question 4 so that after accepting all the names it will ask the user to key in a student-number and then display the name of that student only.

72. Using Tables - Single Dimensional (continued)

Usually a table has to have more than one column - for example information might be held about ten students - but for each one, the name, address and subject studied might be required. This makes the table a little more complicated.

The Data Division entry might be as follows:

```
01  STUDENT-TABLE.
      05  STUDENT-DETAILS OCCURS 10.
```

but each student-details breaks down into three separate pieces of information - so continue:

```
            10 STUDENT-NAME PIC X(30).
            10 STUDENT-ADDRESS PIC X(60).
            10 STUDENT-SUBJECT PIC X(20).
```

If you want to refer all the information about - say - the third student entered then this can be done by asking for STUDENT-DETAILS(3) - e.g.

DISPLAY STUDENT-DETAILS(3).

If, however, just the name of the third student is required - then this will be found by talking about STUDENT-NAME(3).

Note that the name of any item within a table must always be followed by a number (or a data item with a numeric value) in brackets - e.g.

STUDENT-SUBJECT(5),
STUDENT-ADDRESS(1),
STUDENT-DETAILS(STUDENT-NUMBER).

Exercises
1.   How many characters are occupied by the details of one student in the above example ?
2.   How much space does the whole table occupy ?
3.   Write a program which will ask for the details of 5 students and store them in an array - then display all the names in a column.
4.   A table in memory has to be used to hold information about 20 employees in a company - name, address, job title, annual salary. Write suitable Data Division entries for this table.

73. Using Tables - Two Dimensional

The following entry sets up space in memory for a table to hold 3 marks for each of four students.

```
DATA DIVISION.
WORKING-STORAGE SECTION.
01 STUDENT-MARK-TABLE.
   05 STUDENT-LINE OCCURS 4.
      10 STUDENT-MARK PIC 999 OCCURS 3.
```

This table might contain data as follows:

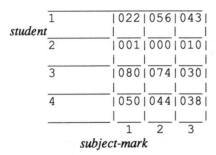

subject-mark

To refer - say - to the second column of the first line (i.e. the second mark for the first student) - then you would use STUDENT-MARK(1,2) - e.g.

    DISPLAY STUDENT-MARK(1,2).

This command would result in **056** being displayed (i.e. the first student's mark for his/her second subject.

To display the whole line for one student - you could use - for example -

    DISPLAY STUDENT-LINE(4).

The data would then be displayed exactly as it is stored (i.e. with no spaces):
050044038

Exercise
Looking at the table above - what would be displayed in response to each of the following commands:
1.   DISPLAY STUDENT-MARK(4,3)
2.   DISPLAY STUDENT-MARK(1,2)
3.   DISPLAY STUDENT-MARK(2,1)
4.   DISPLAY STUDENT-LINE(1)
5.   DISPLAY STUDENT-MARK-TABLE

74.   *Using Tables - Two Dimensional (continued)*

Example Program - asks the user to key in 3 marks for each of 5 students and then displays the table.

```
IDENTIFICATION DIVISION.
PROGRAM-ID.  STUDENT-RESULTS-PROG.

ENVIRONMENT DIVISION.

DATA DIVISION.
WORKING-STORAGE SECTION.
01 STUDENT-RESULTS-TABLE.
      05 STUDENT-RESULT-LINE OCCURS 5.
         10 STUDENT-MARK PIC 999 OCCURS 3.
01    STUDENT-NUM    PIC 9.
01    SUBJECT-NUM    PIC 9.
PROCEDURE DIVISION.
PROCESS-RESULTS-MAIN.
      PERFORM FILL-TABLE
      PERFORM DISPLAY-TABLE
      STOP RUN.
FILL-TABLE.
      PERFORM FILL-LINE VARYING STUDENT-NUM FROM 1 BY 1
      UNTIL STUDENT-NUM > 5.
FILL-LINE.
      DISPLAY 'STUDENT NUMBER - ', STUDENT-NUM
      PERFORM GET-MARK VARYING SUBJECT-NUM FROM 1 BY 1
            UNTIL SUBJECT-NUM > 3.
GET-MARK.
      DISPLAY 'SUBJECT NUMBER - ', SUBJECT-NUM
      ACCEPT STUDENT-MARK(STUDENT-NUM, SUBJECT-NUM).

DISPLAY-TABLE.
      PERFORM DISPLAY-LINE VARYING STUDENT-NUM FROM 1 BY
      1 UNTIL STUDENT-NUM > 5.
DISPLAY-LINE.
      DISPLAY STUDENT-NUM,' '
       STUDENT-MARK (STUDENT-NUM, 1),' '
       STUDENT-MARK (STUDENT-NUM, 2),' '
       STUDENT-MARK (STUDENT-NUM, 3).
```

Exercises
1.   Alter the second half of the above program so that instead of displaying the whole table - it will ask the user to key in which student-number and subject number is required and just display the relevant result.
2.   Alter the program so that it will deal with results for 10 students but only two subjects.

75. *Using REDEFINES*

It is possible to describe a single area of storage in two different ways using REDEFINES.

This is particularly useful to allow a reference table to be set up already containing data.

e.g.(1)

```
01 ALPHABET PIC X(26) VALUE
        'ABCDEFGHIJKLMNOPQRSTUVWXYZ'.
01 LETTER-TABLE REDEFINES ALPHABET.
    05 LETTER-OF-ALPHABET PIC X OCCURS 26.
```

This means that ALPHABET and LETTER-TABLE both refer to the same area of memory. So, DISPLAY ALPHABET and DISPLAY LETTER-TABLE will have the same effect.

A particular letter of the alphabet can be displayed by reference to its position in the table - e.g. DISPLAY LETTER-OF-ALPHABET(5) will cause an 'E' to appear on the screen.

e.g.(2)

```
01 DAYS-OF-WEEK PIC X VALUE 'SUNMONTUEWEDTHUFRISAT'.
01 DAY-TABLE REDEFINES DAYS-OF-WEEK.
    05 DAY-NAME PIC X(3) OCCURS 7.
```

In this case, DAY-TABLE and DAYS-OF-WEEK both refer to the same area of storage. A day of the week can be displayed by reference to its position in the table - e.g. DISPLAY DAY-NAME(2).

Note
REDEFINES cannot be used with 01 Level entries in the FILE SECTION. It is possible instead to simply define a number of different record types for the same file. (See Lesson 59).

Exercises
1.   Set up a table of the months of the year (containing the first three letters of each month).
2.   Write a program which will display the name of the month when its number is keyed in.

76. Revision Test

1. What is the purpose of the file defined with SD in a program which carries out sorting ? (Lesson 69)
2. A file called STOCK-DATA contains unsorted information. Write a statement which will sort this in ascending order of STOCK-NUMBER and give an output file called SORTED-STOCK-DATA. The work file should be called WORK-FILE-STOCK. (69)
3. Should the files that will be used be open or closed before you use the SORT command ? (69)
4. Write a statement which will tell the computer to carry out a paragraph called PROCESS-STOCK-ITEM 20 times - keeping count of the number of times in a data item called STOCK-ITEM-COUNT. Write a suitable data description for STOCK-ITEM-COUNT. (70)
5. Explain how the following statement will work:
    PERFORM PRODUCE-STUDENT-REPORT
        VARYING STUDENT-NUMBER FROM 5 BY 5
        UNTIL STUDENT-NUMBER > 1000.
    Write a suitable data description for STUDENT-NUMBER. (70)
6. Explain the following:
    ```
    01   STOCK-TABLE.
        05 STOCK-ITEM PIC X(30) OCCURS 10.
    ```
    How much memory does this table occupy ? (71)
7. Write a suitable data description for a table to contain the names of 20 students. (71)
8. Explain the following:
    ```
    01   STOCK-TABLE.
        05   STOCK-ITEM OCCURS 10.
            10   STOCK-ITEM-NUM PIC 999.
            10   STOCK-ITEM-DESCR PIC X(30).
    ```
    How much memory does this table occupy ? (72)
9. Write a suitable data description for a table to contain the names and ages of 20 students. (72)
10. Explain the following:
    ```
    01   STOCK-TABLE.
        05 STOCK-LINE OCCURS 10.
            10 STOCK-COLUMN PIC X(20) OCCURS 5.
    ```
    How much memory does this table occupy ?
11. Write a suitable data description for a table to contain the marks for 5 subjects for 20 students - the table to be referenced by the student-number and subject-number. (73)

77. *Indexed Sequential Files - Introduction*

An Indexed Sequential File is organised so that it is easy to find information quickly without the computer having to search through the whole file.

The file includes a number of indexes and the computer can look at these to find exactly where in the file to find the record - in much the same way that you would use a library catalogue to find a book rather than looking along all the shelves.

This is ideal for files which are used for reference - such as in an airline booking system or a library catalogue: it would be very slow to have to hunt all the way through the files in order to find a particular flight or a particular library book - so an ordinary sequential file would not be suitable.

It is possible to insert new records into an Indexed Sequential File - so it is not necessary to copy a whole file across to a new one just to add a single record (as would be the case with a sequential file) as the system leaves space for later insertions; likewise, it is easy to alter a record in place without writing the whole file out again, or to delete a record.

Again this is very suitable for systems such as travel or theatre booking where information has to be changed frequently and it would be inefficient to copy out a whole file again just to alter information about one or two seats.

When setting up an Indexed Sequential File in the first place, the programmer has to specify which field will be used as the key field - e.g. a student file might use student name, or number as the key field - this is the item which will be looked up in the index in order to find a record.

Note that some operating systems automatically set up a properly indexed file with sufficient space when your program runs: with others however you will have to set up a template for the file (i.e. give information about it) using a utility program before running the program which will use the file.

Exercise
1. List 5 applications for which an Indexed Sequential File would be very suitable - give reasons.
2. List 2 applications where an Indexed Sequential File would be less suitable than a Sequential File - give reasons.
3. Give suitable key fields for each of the following files - employee records, an estate agent's file of houses for sale, student records, list of computers owned by a company.

78. *Writing to an Indexed Sequential File*

Example

```
.....
ENVIRONMENT DIVISION.
INPUT-OUTPUT SECTION.
FILE-CONTROL.
SELECT STUDENT-FILE ASSIGN TO 'STUDENTS'
     ORGANIZATION IS INDEXED
     ACCESS MODE IS RANDOM
     RECORD KEY IS STUDENT-SURNAME.

DATA DIVISION.
FILE SECTION.
FD    STUDENT-FILE.
01    STUDENT-RECORD.
      05 STUDENT-SURNAME PIC X(20).
      05 STUDENT-FIRST-NAMES PIC X(30).
      05 STUDENT-COURSE-CODE PIC X(5).
WORKING-STORAGE SECTION.
01    FINISHED-IND PIC X VALUE 'N'.

PROCEDURE DIVISION.
PROCESS-STUDENT-FILE-MAIN.
     OPEN OUTPUT STUDENT-FILE
     PERFORM PROCESS-STUDENT-RECORD
          UNTIL FINISHED-IND = 'Y'
     CLOSE STUDENT-FILE
     STOP RUN.
PROCESS-STUDENT-RECORD.
     PERFORM GET-STUDENT-DATA
     PERFORM WRITE-STUDENT-DATA
     PERFORM CHECK-IF-FINISHED.
GET-STUDENT-DATA.
     DISPLAY 'SURNAME ?' ACCEPT STUDENT-SURNAME
     DISPLAY 'FIRST NAMES ?' ACCEPT STUDENT-FIRST-NAMES
     DISPLAY 'COURSE CODE ?'
     ACCEPT STUDENT-COURSE-CODE.
WRITE-STUDENT-DATA.
     WRITE STUDENT-RECORD
          INVALID KEY PERFORM ERROR-ROUTINE
     END-WRITE.
```

Write and Read statements must contain a command saying what the computer should do if the key given is invalid (e.g. if two records have the same key).

```
CHECK-IF-FINISHED.
     DISPLAY 'FINISHED ?'
     ACCEPT FINISHED-IND.
ERROR-ROUTINE.
     DISPLAY 'INVALID KEY - RECORD NOT SAVED'.
```

Exercise

Write a program which allows a staff-file to be built up containing each employee's surname, first names, address, job title, department, salary.

140

79. Reading from an Indexed Sequential File

In order to read from an Indexed Sequential File it is necessary to place the key for the record you want in the appropriate field before attempting to read. The program will then find the record which has that key field.

Example

. . . .
The Environment Division and Data Division for this program are the same as for the example program in the previous lesson with the addition of 01 ERROR-IND PIC 9 in the Working-Storage Section.

```
PROCEDURE DIVISION.
PROCESS-STUDENT-FILE-MAIN.
      OPEN INPUT STUDENT-FILE
      PERFORM PROCESS-STUDENT-RECORD
          UNTIL FINISHED-IND = 'Y'
      CLOSE STUDENT-FILE
      STOP RUN.
PROCESS-STUDENT-RECORD.
      PERFORM GET-STUDENT-SURNAME
      PERFORM GET-RECORD
      PERFORM DISPLAY-RECORD
      PERFORM CHECK-IF-FINISHED.
GET-STUDENT-SURNAME.
      DISPLAY 'SURNAME ? '
      ACCEPT STUDENT-SURNAME.
GET-RECORD.
      PERFORM WITH TEST AFTER UNTIL ERROR-IND = 0

          READ STUDENT-FILE
          INVALID KEY
              DISPLAY 'INVALID KEY - PLEASE RETYPE'
              ACCEPT STUDENT-SURNAME
              MOVE 1 TO ERROR-IND
          NOT INVALID KEY
              MOVE 0 TO ERROR-IND
          END-READ
```
If the key is invalid, then the computer will display a message and set the field ERROR-IND to 1. If the key is not invalid, ERROR-IND will be set to 0.

```
      END-PERFORM.
```
ERROR-IND is checked and if it has been set to 1, then the routine is PERFORMed again.

```
DISPLAY-RECORD.
      DISPLAY STUDENT-SURNAME ,' ', STUDENT-FIRST-NAMES
      DISPLAY 'COURSE CODE ', STUDENT-COURSE-CODE.
CHECK-IF-FINISHED.
      DISPLAY 'FINISHED ? Y/N' ACCEPT FINISHED-IND.
```

Exercise
Write a program which will allow the user to specify an employee by surname - then retrieve and display all the data about him/her (use the data file created in the previous exercise).

141

80. *Indexed Sequential Files - Reading and Writing*

One of the advantages of an Indexed Sequential File is that it is possible to find the required record, read it, alter it, and write the altered record back into position.

Example

......

The Environment Division and Data Division for this program are the same as for the example program in the previous lesson.

```
PROCEDURE DIVISION.
PROCESS-STUDENT-FILE-MAIN.
     OPEN I-O STUDENT-FILE
     PERFORM PROCESS-STUDENT-RECORD
         UNTIL FINISHED-IND = 'Y'
     CLOSE STUDENT-FILE
     STOP RUN.

PROCESS-STUDENT-RECORD.
     PERFORM GET-STUDENT-SURNAME
     PERFORM GET-RECORD
     PERFORM DISPLAY-RECORD
     PERFORM GET-ALTERATION
     PERFORM WRITE-RECORD
     PERFORM CHECK-IF-FINISHED.
GET-STUDENT-SURNAME.
     DISPLAY 'SURNAME ? ' ACCEPT STUDENT-SURNAME.
GET-RECORD.
     PERFORM WITH TEST AFTER UNTIL ERROR-IND = 0
         READ STUDENT-FILE
         INVALID KEY
             DISPLAY 'INVALID KEY - PLEASE RETYPE'
             ACCEPT STUDENT-SURNAME
             MOVE 1 TO ERROR-IND
         NOT INVALID KEY
             MOVE 0 TO ERROR-IND
         END-READ
     END-PERFORM.
DISPLAY-RECORD.
     DISPLAY STUDENT-SURNAME, ' ', STUDENT-FIRST-NAMES
     DISPLAY 'COURSE CODE ', STUDENT-COURSE-CODE.
GET-ALTERATION.
     DISPLAY 'NEW COURSE CODE '
     ACCEPT  STUDENT-COURSE-CODE.
WRITE-RECORD.
     REWRITE STUDENT-RECORD
         INVALID KEY
         DISPLAY 'ERROR INDICATED - SUGGEST FINISH'
     END-REWRITE.
CHECK-IF-FINISHED.
     DISPLAY 'FINISHED ? Y/N'  ACCEPT FINISHED-IND.
```

Exercise

Write a program which will allow records in the employee file created in the previous lessons to be altered.

81. Indexed Sequential Files - Dynamic Access

Sometimes it is useful to have the option of either chosing a particular record from the key or simply reading through the file sequentially perhaps starting at a particular point.

To do this, the Access Mode has to be specified as *Dynamic* rather than *Random*.

Example

```
. . . . .
ENVIRONMENT DIVISION.
INPUT-OUTPUT SECTION.
FILE-CONTROL.
SELECT STUDENT-FILE ASSIGN TO 'STUDENTS'
      ORGANIZATION IS INDEXED
      ACCESS MODE IS DYNAMIC
      RECORD KEY IS STUDENT-SURNAME.

DATA DIVISION.
FILE SECTION.
FD    STUDENT-FILE.
01    STUDENT-RECORD.
      05 STUDENT-SURNAME PIC X(20).
      05 STUDENT-FIRST-NAMES PIC X(30).
      05 STUDENT-COURSE-CODE PIC X(5).
WORKING-STORAGE SECTION.
01    EOF-INDICATOR   PIC X VALUE SPACE.
01    ERROR-IND       PIC 9.
PROCEDURE DIVISION.
PROCESS-STUDENT-MAIN.
      OPEN INPUT STUDENT-FILE
      PERFORM GET-START-KEY
      PERFORM READ-RECORD
      PERFORM PROCESS-STUDENT-RECORD
            UNTIL EOF-INDICATOR = 'E'
      CLOSE STUDENT-FILE
      STOP RUN.
GET-START-KEY.
      PERFORM WITH TEST AFTER UNTIL ERROR-IND = 0
            DISPLAY 'CHARACTER FOR START OF BROWSE'
            ACCEPT STUDENT-SURNAME
            START STUDENT-FILE KEY IS NOT LESS THAN
                  STUDENT-SURNAME
            INVALID KEY
                  DISPLAY 'ERROR - PLEASE RETYPE'
                  MOVE 1 TO ERROR-IND
            NOT INVALID KEY
                  MOVE 0 TO ERROR-IND
            END-START
      END-PERFORM.
```
(e.g. if 'C' were keyed in, then the next READ would START with the first record whose surname started with the letter C or higher)

```
PROCESS-STUDENT-RECORD.
      PERFORM DISPLAY-RECORD
      PERFORM READ-RECORD.
```

143

```
READ-RECORD.
      READ STUDENT-FILE NEXT RECORD
            AT END MOVE 'E' TO EOF-INDICATOR
      END-READ.
DISPLAY-RECORD.
      DISPLAY STUDENT-SURNAME,
      DISPLAY STUDENT-FIRST-NAMES
      DISPLAY 'COURSE ', STUDENT-COURSE-CODE.
```

Note that although the above program only makes use of sequential reads - if Dynamic Access Mode is used, then it is possible to switch from one type of READ to the other.

Exercise

Write a program which will allow the user to browse through the employee file starting at a certain point.

82. Worked Project 5 - Using an Indexed Sequential File

Produce a program which will allow a user to keep up-to-date records on students following a City and Guilds programming course. During the course the students each take 5 assessments in each of their subjects - these assessments may be taken at any time (each student taking an assessment when he/she is ready). Each assessment will earn either a pass or a fail - and may be retaken if necessary until passed. If all assessments are passed then the course is passed and the computer will issue a report stating that a certificate should be issued.

Each student may take up to 4 computing subjects.

The file will also need to store personal information about each student - name, address, date-of-birth, nationality, together with the student's college student number.

A new student can join the course at any time in the year.

The teacher should on entering the system be presented with a suitable menu giving the options of:

1. adding a student;
2. amending the personal details of a student;
3. recording an assessment result (or changing a fail to a pass after a resit);
4. viewing the record of a particular student;
5. producing a report on all students who should have a certificate and in what subject (remembering to avoid the possibility of a student receiving two certificates for the same subject);
6. finishing.

If a number other than 1 - 6 is keyed then the program should display an error message and return to the menu.

TACKLING THE PROJECT

As the file is to be kept as up-to-date as possible this means that each transaction should be entered as it occurs (e.g immediately a student passes an assessment - this should be recorded).

This means that at any one time only a small number of records will be looked at. For this reason it would be inefficient to use a sequential file as in order to look at a particular record it would be necessary to go through the whole lot and in order to add or alter a record the whole file would have to be rewritten.

An Indexed Sequential File would be ideal as any record can be viewed or amended without going through the whole file - but the option remains of going through the whole file sequentially (as would be required by option 5 above).

DESIGN

The program can be seen as a control section consisting of the menu processing and a number of sub-programs each carrying out a particular piece of processing.

The main section of the program will consist of opening the file, carrying out processing of the files and finally closing the files - shown on the structure diagram below:

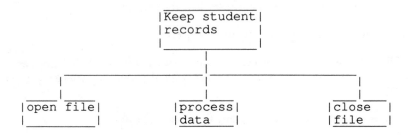

Processing the data will consist of presenting a menu, accepting a choice, carrying out that choice then returning to the menu until the user indicates that he/she has finished. This is a repetitive task - so we need to think of a name which will summarise the whole task and can be represented by a single rectangle - e.g. *process menu routine*.

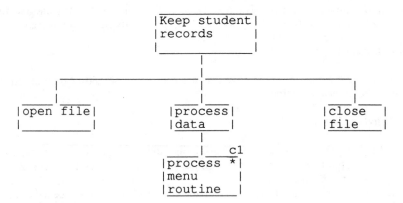

c1 - until choice = 6

The job of processing the menu routine will break down into the sequence listed above:

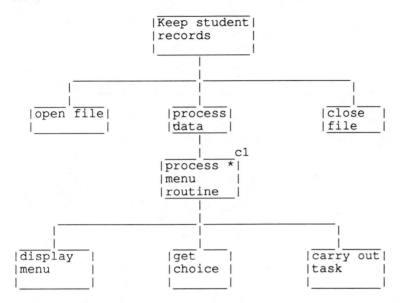

c1 - until choice = 6

Carrying out the task will break down into a selection as the computer has 6 possible courses of action:

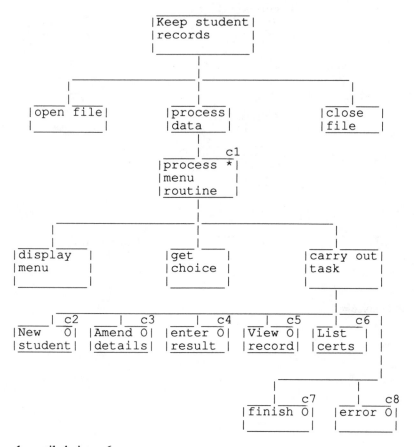

c1 - until choice = 6
c2 - if choice = 1
c3 - if choice = 2
c4 - if choice = 3
c5 - if choice = 4
c6 - if choice = 5
c7 - if choice = 6
c8 - if choice < 1 or choice >5

It is sensible at this point to write the routine to carry out this control section of the program and test it - using 'dummy routines' which simply display a message proving that the proper routine has been entered (e.g. if the user chooses option 1 - then a message could be displayed stating 'New student routine'). These dummy routines can be replaced with the full sub-programs later on.

The record for each student will need to hold personal details, results for 4 subjects, each having 5 assessments to record as 'P' or 'F' or a space, and in addition an indicator is needed for each subject to show whether the certificate has already been issued - otherwise the student will get a new certificate every time the teacher asks for option 5.

```
FILE SECTION.
FD STUDENT-FILE.
01 STUDENT-RECORD.
   05  PERSONAL-DETAILS.
      10    STUDENT-NUMBER PIC X(7).
      10    SURNAME        PIC  X(20).
      10    FIRST-NAMES    PIC X(30).
      10    STUDENT-ADDRESS    PIC X(60).
      10    NATIONALITY    PIC  X(20).
      10    DATE-OF-BIRTH  PIC 9(6).
   05 COURSE-DETAILS.
      10 SUBJECT-DETAILS  OCCURS 4 TIMES.
         15 SUBJECT-NAME      PIC X(20).
         15 ASSESSMENT-RESULTS OCCURS 5 TIMES.
            20 ASSESSMENT-RESULT PIC X.
         15 CERTIFICATE-ISSUED-FLAG PIC X.
```

Exercise
How long is this record ?

For option 5 the computer will be required to read the file sequentially, so an end-of-file flag is needed.
A field to hold the user's choice is also needed.

```
WORKING-STORAGE SECTION.
01    EOF-INDICATOR  PIC X VALUE SPACE.
01    CHOICE         PIC 9.
```

PARAGRAPHS

From the Structure Diagram so far - the following paragraphs could be used:

PROCESS-STUDENT-RECORDS-MAIN.
OPEN-FILE.
PROCESS-FILE.
CLOSE-FILE.

PROCESS-MENU-ROUTINE.

DISPLAY-MENU.
GET-CHOICE.
PROCESS-TASK-CHOSEN.
PROCESS-NEW-STUDENT.
PROCESS-ALTER-DETAILS.
PROCESS-RECORD-RESULT.
PROCESS-VIEW-STUDENT.

```
PROCESS-REPORT-CERTIFICATES.
PROCESS-END.
PROCESS-INVALID-CHOICE.
```

THE PROGRAM CODE

Looking at the top layer of the structure diagram - three procedures are called from the main paragraph:

```
PROCESS-STUDENT-RECORDS-MAIN.
      PERFORM OPEN-FILE
      PERFORM PROCESS-FILE
      PERFORM CLOSE-FILE
      STOP RUN.
```

The file needs to open for either input or output as it is required to read, write or amend records.

```
OPEN-FILE.
      OPEN I-O STUDENT-FILE.
```

Processing the file breaks down into repetitively carrying out the menu-display, getting the choice, processing the choice - summarised as

```
PROCESS-FILE.
      PERFORM PROCESS-MENU-ROUTINE UNTIL CHOICE = 6.

CLOSE-FILE.
      CLOSE STUDENT-FILE.
```

As we have already said - processing the menu routine is a sequence:

```
PROCESS-MENU-ROUTINE.
      PERFORM DISPLAY-MENU
      PERFORM GET-CHOICE
      PERFORM PROCESS-TASK-CHOSEN.
```

Fill in the detailed commands to display the menu as required:

```
DISPLAY-MENU.
      DISPLAY '                   MENU'
      DISPLAY 'INPUT NEW STUDENT             1'
      DISPLAY 'AMEND PERSONAL DETAILS        2'
      DISPLAY 'ENTER RESULT                  3'
      DISPLAY 'VIEW STUDENT RECORD           4'
      DISPLAY 'REPORT ON CERTIFICATES DUE    5'
      DISPLAY 'FINISH                        6'
      DISPLAY 'ENTER CHOICE :'.
GET-CHOICE.
```

```
        ACCEPT CHOICE.

PROCESS-TASK-CHOSEN.
        EVALUATE CHOICE
                WHEN 1 PERFORM PROCESS-NEW-STUDENT
                WHEN 2 PERFORM PROCESS-ALTER-DETAILS
                WHEN 3 PERFORM PROCESS-RECORD-RESULT
                WHEN 4 PERFORM PROCESS-VIEW-STUDENT-RECORD
                WHEN 5 PERFORM PROCESS-REPORT-CERTIFICATES
                WHEN 6 PERFORM PROCESS-END
                WHEN OTHER PERFORM PROCESS-INVALID-CHOICE
        END-EVALUATE.
```

It remains to write the individual procedures to carry out the user's choice - but first the control routine should be tested. If the program is run as it is, it will not be possible to see whether the selections are being made properly, so a command in each routine to state which routine is being run will aid testing and can be removed later.

```
PROCESS-NEW-STUDENT.
        DISPLAY 'NEW STUDENT ROUTINE'.
PROCESS-ALTER-DETAILS.
        DISPLAY 'ALTER ROUTINE'.
PROCESS-RECORD-RESULT.
        DISPLAY 'RESULTS ROUTINE'.
PROCESS-VIEW-STUDENT-RECORD.
        DISPLAY 'VIEW STUDENTS'.
PROCESS-REPORT-CERTIFICATES.
        DISPLAY 'CERTIFICATES'.
PROCESS-END.
        DISPLAY 'END'.
PROCESS-INVALID-CHOICE.
        DISPLAY 'ERROR'.
```

An *IDENTIFICATION DIVISION* and *ENVIRONMENT DIVISION* have to be added:

```
IDENTIFICATION DIVISION.
PROGRAM-ID. STUDENT-RECORDS.

ENVIRONMENT DIVISION.
INPUT-OUTPUT SECTION.
FILE-CONTROL.
        SELECT STUDENT-FILE ASSIGN TO 'STUDENTS'
        ORGANIZATION IS INDEXED
        ACCESS MODE IS RANDOM
        RECORD KEY IS STUDENT-NUMBER.
```

TESTING

Ensure that each condition is tested - by trying out all the menu options.

Make sure that the user is returned to the menu after each choice except option 6.

Check that the menu is displayed as required.

Looking at the disk directory - a file called 'students' should have been created but will not contain any data.

Each sub-program can be designed as if it were a program in itself, provided that you bear in mind that certain tasks will be carried out by the main routine - and certain data is shared - so will not have to be redefined.

The job of opening and closing the file will - in this case - be carried out by the main procedure.

So the job of adding a student consists simply of getting the data from the user and writing it to file - so the main structure diagram will extend:

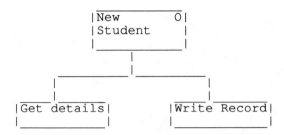

It is also desirable to take account of what will happen in the event of an invalid key - such as allocating the same number to two students:

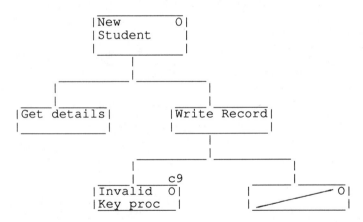

c9 - if invalid key

PARAGRAPHS

GET-STUDENT-DETAILS.
WRITE-RECORD.
INVALID-KEY-ROUTINE.

153

PROGRAM CODE

The contents of **PROCESS-NEW-STUDENT** changes:

```
PROCESS-NEW-STUDENT.
     PERFORM GET-STUDENT-DETAILS
     PERFORM WRITE-RECORD.


GET-STUDENT-DETAILS.
     DISPLAY 'STUDENT NUMBER ?'
     ACCEPT STUDENT-NUMBER
     DISPLAY 'SURNAME ?'
     ACCEPT SURNAME
     DISPLAY 'FIRST NAMES ?'
     ACCEPT FIRST-NAMES
     DISPLAY 'ADDRESS ?'
     ACCEPT STUDENT-ADDRESS
     DISPLAY 'DATE OF BIRTH ?'
     ACCEPT DATE-OF-BIRTH
     DISPLAY 'FIRST SUBJECT STUDIED ?'
     ACCEPT SUBJECT-NAME(1)
     DISPLAY 'SECOND SUBJECT STUDIED ?'
     ACCEPT SUBJECT-NAME(2)
     DISPLAY 'THIRD SUBJECT STUDIED ?'
     ACCEPT SUBJECT-NAME(3)
     DISPLAY 'FOURTH SUBJECT STUDIED ?'
     ACCEPT SUBJECT-NAME(4).


WRITE-RECORD.
     WRITE STUDENT-RECORD
     INVALID KEY
          PERFORM INVALID-KEY-ROUTINE
     END-WRITE.

INVALID-KEY-ROUTINE.
     DISPLAY 'INVALID KEY - data not stored'.
```

TESTING

Points to check are
1.   that the prompts are displayed correctly;

2.   that an error message is displayed if the key is invalid (e.g. two students with the same number);

3.   that the data is correctly stored on disk - but this cannot be easily checked until a routine to read the file and display it has been written.

Exercise
Design and code the remaining procedures.

83.   Sequential File Update

One of the commonest problems to deal with is bringing a sequential file up-to-date with new information.

As it is not possible to add new information directly into the middle of a sequential file - it is necessary to create a new up-to-date file.

This is generally done by first putting all the changes into a *transaction file* (i.e. a file of changes) - sorting them into order and then using data from the old main file together with the transaction file to create a new main file.

For example the main student file for a class contains 7 students' records showing their names and ages:

```
ANDERSON    20
CHOWDURY    19
DAVIS       21
EDWARDS     17
OLADEDJU    18
ROBERTS     19
WILLIAMS    20
```

3 new students join the class, 2 leave and 1 is found to have his age recorded incorrectly - so a transaction file is created containing the name, age if necessary and transaction type (i.e. Insert in the file, Delete from the file or Amend a Record):

```
ROGERS      18     I
DAVIS              D
ANDREWS     19     I
WILLIAMS           D
CHENG       20     I
ROBERTS     20     A
```

This needs to be sorted into order - before it can be used to update the main file:

```
ANDREWS     19     I
CHENG       20     I
DAVIS              D
ROBERTS     20     A
ROGERS      18     I
WILLIAMS           D
```

Now the update program will use information from the main file together with the transaction file to create a new main file:

```
ANDERSON    20
ANDREWS     19
CHENG       20
CHOWDURY    19
EDWARDS     17
OLADEDJU    18
ROBERTS     20
ROGERS      18
```

84. Worked Project 6 - Sequential File Update

Program 1

Produce a program which will allow a main student-file to be created with a record layout as follows:

```
01 STUDENT-RECORD.
     05 STUDENT-NAME.
          10 STUDENT-SURNAME PIC X(20).
          10 STUDENT-INITIALS PIC X(2).
     05 STUDENT-AGE        PIC 99.
```

When you run the program take care to key your data in order (of name).

Program 2

Produce a program which will allow a student transaction file to be created with a record layout as follows:

```
01 STUDENT-TRANSACTION-RECORD.
     05 STUDENT-NAME.
          10 STUDENT-SURNAME PIC X(20).
          10 STUDENT-INITIALS PIC X(2).
     05 STUDENT-AGE        PIC 99.
     05 TRANSACTION-TYPE PIC X.
```

Program 3

Produce a program which will take the unsorted transaction file created by program 2, sort it and use it to update the main student-file.

Exercise
Produce programs 1 and 2.

Program 3

DESIGN
The program can be seen as consisting of two main sections (which could in fact be written as two separate programs):
1. the sort;
2. the update.

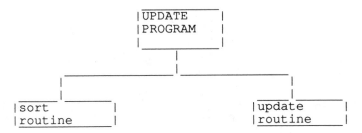

The sort routine does not need to be broken down any further - remember that the SORT verb in COBOL carries out all the file handling tasks required.

The update routine breaks down into opening the files, processing the files and closing the files.

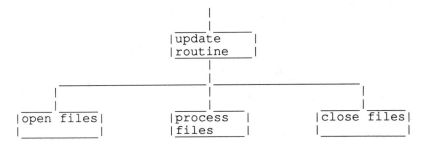

Processing the files can be seen as repeatedly processing a single record.

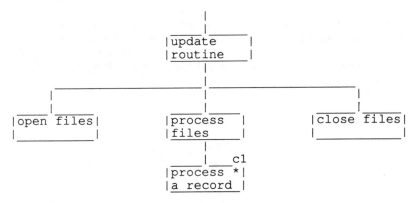

c1 - until end-of-main-file and end-of-transaction-file.

The task of processing a record will be different according to what has to be done to the record.

There are four possibilities:
1.   no change;
2.   insertion;
3.   amendment;
4.   deletion.

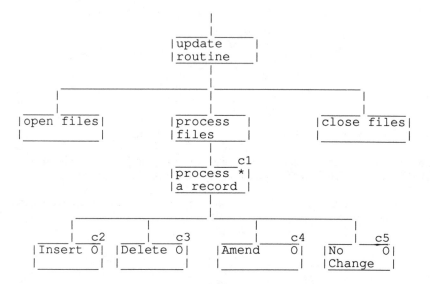

c1 - until end-of-main-file and end-of-transaction-file.
c2 - if (transaction type = 'I' AND transaction record key < main-file record key) OR end-of-main-file indicator is set

If a transaction record is read which has to be inserted, the program has to keep reading (and writing) records from the main file until it is the right place to insert the new record. This will be when a main-file record is read which has a higher key than the transaction record; the transaction record can then be written before it in the new file.

c3 - if transaction type = 'D' and transaction record key = master-file record key. *(i.e. the program has found the master-file record which is to be deleted).*
c4 - if transaction type = 'A' and transaction record key = master-file record key.
c5 - all other valid situations - i.e. the old master record does not require any changes and can be copied to the new file.

In order to decide what has to be done at any point the program will have to have access to one record from the main file and one from the transaction file for comparison purposes - so a record from each could be read before the main processing starts - having the additional advantage that it is a check for ends of files.

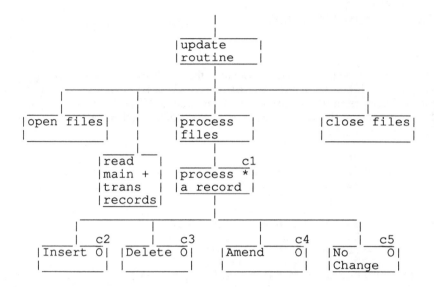

An Insertion consists of writing the transaction record to the new main file followed by reading another record from the transaction file so there is always one in main memory to compare with the main-file record held there.

A Deletion consists of reading another record from the old-main file and one from the transaction file (no record is written to the new main file).

An Amendment consists of making the change to the main-file record and writing it to the new main-file, then reading a record from the old-main file and one from the transaction file.

All other (valid) circumstances consist of simply writing the old main-file record to the new main-file and reading another from the old-main file.

PARAGRAPHS
MAIN.

SORT-ROUTINE.
UPDATE-ROUTINE.

OPEN-FILES.
PROCESS-FILES.
CLOSE-FILES.

PROCESS-RECORD.

INSERT-RECORD.
DELETE-RECORD.
AMEND-RECORD.
UNCHANGED-RECORD.
READ-TRANSACTION-FILE.
READ-MAIN-FILE.
ALTER-RECORD.
WRITE-TO-NEW-MAIN-FILE.

DATA

The File Section will need to take account of the SORT routine and the update.

Three files will be used for the Sort routine - including a work-file, the original unsorted transaction file and the new sorted transaction file.

The third of these files will also be used for the update together with an old main-file and a new main-file.

```
FILE SECTION.
SD STUDENT-TRANS-WORK-FILE.
01 W-STUDENT-TRANSACTION-RECORD.
      05 W-STUDENT-NAME.
          10 W-STUDENT-SURNAME PIC X(20).
          10 W-STUDENT-INITIALS PIC X(2).
      05 W-STUDENT-AGE       PIC 99.
      05 W-TRANSACTION-TYPE PIC X.
FD UNSORTED-STUDENT-TRANS-FILE.
01 UNSORTED-STUDENT-TRANS-REC PIC X(25).
FD SORTED-STUDENT-TRANS-FILE.
01 STUDENT-TRANSACTION-RECORD.
      03 STUDENT-TRANSACTION-DETAILS.
        05 STUDENT-NAME.
          10 STUDENT-SURNAME PIC X(20).
          10 STUDENT-INITIALS PIC X(2).
        05 STUDENT-AGE       PIC 99.
      03   TRANSACTION-TYPE PIC X.
FD    STUDENT-OLD-MAIN-FILE.
01 OLD-MAIN-STUDENT-RECORD.
      05 OLD-MAIN-STUDENT-NAME.
          10 OLD-MAIN-STUDENT-SURNAME PIC X(20).
          10 OLD-MAIN-STUDENT-INITIALS PIC X(2).
      05 OLD-MAIN-STUDENT-AGE        PIC 99.
FD    STUDENT-NEW-MAIN-FILE.
01 NEW-MAIN-STUDENT-RECORD PIC X(24).
```

The Working-Storage Section should have an end-of-file indicator for each of the two files and could use Level 88 to express the actual end-of-file conditions:

```
01    END-OF-OLD-MAIN-FILE-IND PIC   X.
      88 END-OF-OLD-MAIN-FILE VALUE 'E'.
01    END-OF-TRANSACTION-FILE-IND PIC X.
      88 END-OF-TRANSACTION-FILE VALUE 'E'.
```

```
MAIN.
      PERFORM SORT-ROUTINE
      PERFORM UPDATE-ROUTINE
      STOP RUN.

SORT-ROUTINE.
      SORT STUDENT-TRANS-WORK-FILE
           ASCENDING KEY W-STUDENT-NAME
           USING UNSORTED-STUDENT-TRANS-FILE
           GIVING SORTED-STUDENT-TRANS-FILE.

UPDATE-ROUTINE.
      PERFORM OPEN-FILES
      PERFORM READ-TRANSACTION-FILE
      PERFORM READ-OLD-MAIN-FILE
      PERFORM PROCESS-FILES
      PERFORM CLOSE-FILES.
```

The remainder of the code relates to the update, so we are only concerned with the two master files and the sorted transaction file.

```
OPEN-FILES.
      OPEN INPUT SORTED-STUDENT-TRANS-FILE
                 STUDENT-OLD-MAIN-FILE
      OPEN OUTPUT STUDENT-NEW-MAIN-FILE.
PROCESS-FILES.
      PERFORM PROCESS-RECORD
           UNTIL END-OF-TRANSACTION-FILE
              AND END-OF-OLD-MAIN-FILE.
CLOSE-FILES.
      CLOSE SORTED-STUDENT-TRANS-FILE
            STUDENT-OLD-MAIN-FILE
            STUDENT-NEW-MAIN-FILE.

PROCESS-RECORD.
      IF TRANSACTION-TYPE = 'I' AND
      (STUDENT-NAME IS LESS THAN
       OLD-MAIN-STUDENT-NAME OR END-OF-OLD-MAIN-FILE)
          PERFORM INSERT-RECORD
      ELSE
        IF TRANSACTION-TYPE = 'D' AND
           STUDENT-NAME = OLD-MAIN-STUDENT-NAME
           PERFORM DELETE-RECORD
        ELSE
          IF TRANSACTION-TYPE = 'A' AND
             STUDENT-NAME = OLD-MAIN-STUDENT-NAME
             PERFORM AMEND-RECORD
          ELSE
             PERFORM UNCHANGED-RECORD
          END-IF
        END-IF
      END-IF.
```

161

```
INSERT-RECORD.
     PERFORM WRITE-TRANS-REC-TO-NEW-MAIN
     PERFORM READ-TRANSACTION-FILE.

DELETE-RECORD.
     PERFORM READ-TRANSACTION-FILE
     PERFORM READ-OLD-MAIN-FILE.

AMEND-RECORD.
     PERFORM WRITE-TRANS-REC-TO-NEW-MAIN
     PERFORM READ-OLD-MAIN-FILE
     PERFORM READ-TRANSACTION-FILE.

UNCHANGED-RECORD.
     PERFORM WRITE-OLD-MAIN-REC-TO-NEW-MAIN
     PERFORM READ-OLD-MAIN-FILE.

READ-TRANSACTION-FILE.
     READ SORTED-STUDENT-TRANS-FILE
          AT END MOVE 'E'
          TO END-OF-TRANSACTION-FILE-IND
     END-READ.

READ-OLD-MAIN-FILE.
     READ STUDENT-OLD-MAIN-FILE
          AT END MOVE 'E'
          TO END-OF-OLD-MAIN-FILE-IND
     END-READ.

WRITE-TRANS-REC-TO-NEW-MAIN.
     MOVE STUDENT-TRANSACTION-DETAILS TO
          NEW-MAIN-STUDENT-RECORD
     WRITE NEW-MAIN-STUDENT-RECORD.

WRITE-OLD-MAIN-REC-TO-NEW-MAIN.
     MOVE OLD-MAIN-STUDENT-RECORD TO
          NEW-MAIN-STUDENT-RECORD
     WRITE NEW-MAIN-STUDENT-RECORD.
```

IDENTIFICATION DIVISION and ENVIRONMENT DIVISION

```
IDENTIFICATION DIVISION.
PROGRAM-ID. STUDENT-RECORDS.

ENVIRONMENT DIVISION.
INPUT-OUTPUT SECTION.
FILE-CONTROL.
     SELECT STUDENT-TRANS-WORK-FILE ASSIGN TO
     'WORKFILE'.
     SELECT UNSORTED-STUDENT-TRANS-FILE ASSIGN TO
     'UNSTRANS'.
     SELECT SORTED-STUDENT-TRANS-FILE ASSIGN TO
     'SRTTRANS'.
     SELECT STUDENT-OLD-MAIN-FILE ASSIGN TO
     'OLDMAIN'.
     SELECT STUDENT-NEW-MAIN-FILE ASSIGN TO
     'NEWMAIN'.
```

TESTING

Check whether the program copes successfully with insertions, deletions and amendments by keying in a set of records in order to Program 1 to create an old main-file, and a set of transaction records (in any order) to Program 2 to create an unsorted transaction file. Run the program and look at the file 'NEWMAIN' and ensure that it is as expected.

e.g.

Records for OLDMAIN

```
name        age
ANDREWS     20
FONDA       20
ROGERS      20
SAMSON      20
VICTOR      20
```

Records for UNSTRANS

```
name        age     transaction type
ANDERSON    20      I
COLLINS     20      I
BLOGGS      20      I
ANDREWS     20      D
FONDA       21      A
```

Expected Output (NEWMAIN)

```
ANDERSON    20
BLOGGS      20
COLLINS     20
FONDA       21
ROGERS      20
SAMSON      20
VICTOR      20
```

Notes:
1. When the program is run - 'unstrans', and 'oldmain' must already be in existence.
2. It is important to ensure that the file 'OLDMAIN' is typed in sequentially (i.e. in alphabetical order of name).
3. The program will not cope with invalid transaction types - e.g. trying to delete or amend a record that does not exist in the old main-file - so ensure that the transactions are all valid before entering them.

85. Using INSPECT

INSPECT .. TALLYING may be used to count the number of times a particular character appears in a word.

e.g.1   INSPECT REPORT-TEXT TALLYING A-COUNT FOR ALL 'A'

will use the data-item A-COUNT to keep count of any 'A's which occur in REPORT-TEXT. (A-COUNT must be defined as numeric and be sufficiently large to contain the count).

It is also possible to count the number of times a group of characters appears.

e.g.2   INSPECT LETTER-TEXT TALLYING AND-COUNT FOR ALL 'AND'

After this statement, AND-COUNT will contain a count of the number of times 'AND' appears in the text. (Note that this will include ANDs which occur as part of other words.)

INSPECT .. REPLACING may be used to look for a particular character and replace it with a different one every time it appears.

e.g.1   INSPECT ITEM-CODE REPLACING ALL 'A' BY 'B'

Again, a group of characters may be specified.

e.g.2   INSPECT LETTER-TEXT REPLACING ALL 'FAIL' BY 'PASS'

INSPECT .. CONVERTING may be used to look for a number of characters from a specific list and replace them with characters from a different list.

e.g.1   INSPECT INVOICE CONVERTING 'ABCD' TO 'WXYZ'

(Each time an 'A' appears it will be converted to a 'W', every 'B' will be turned into an 'X' and so on.)

e.g.2   INSPECT LETTER-TEXT CONVERTING
       'abcdefghijklmnopqrstuvwxyz'
          TO 'ABCDEFGHIJKLMNOPQRSTUVWXYZ'

(Every 'a' will be converted to 'A', etc.)

Exercise
Write a program which will allow a user to type in a message, then carry out the following: a) count the number of spaces; b) count the number of times the word 'THE' appears'; c) turn all capital letters to small letters; d) convert the message into code on the basis that an 'A' should be represented by a 'C' , a 'B' by a 'D', etc. 'Y' should be represented by 'A' and 'Z' by 'B'.

86.   Reference Modification

Reference Modification allows the programmer to refer to part of a data-item rather than the whole item.

For example if MONTH-OF-YEAR is defined as PIC X(20), then

MONTH-OF-YEAR(1:2) refers to the first two letters,

MONTH-OF-YEAR(3:5) refers to the five letters beginning with the third, and so on.

If a data item COMPANY-NAME is defined as PIC X(30) and contains the name ABC COMPUTING P.L.C. then

DISPLAY COMPANY-NAME(1:3) will display 3 letters starting with the first - in this case 'ABC' will appear on the screen.

DISPLAY COMPANY-NAME(2:4) will display 4 letters starting with the second - so 'BC C' should appear.

The starting position and number of characters may themselves be variable and held within other data-items.

The following code will allow the user to decide which letters of the company name, he/she wants to display.

```
DISPLAY 'Starting position ?' ACCEPT X
DISPLAY 'Number of letters ?' ACCEPT Y
DISPLAY COMPANY-NAME (X:Y)
```

(X and Y should have been defined as numeric data-items of a suitable length).

Exercises
1.   Write a program which will use reference modification to search for a space and then display its position in the field.
2.   Write a program which will ask for the name of a student, his/her course, and the date, then form an identity code - made up of the first three letters of the surname followed by the first two letters of the course name and the year of starting the course. *(Hint: MOVE* the relevant data from surname, course-name, etc to the relevant positions in the ID-CODE).

87.   Calling Sub-programs

CALL works in a similar way to PERFORM. However, while PERFORM is an instruction to carry out a separate paragraph or section, CALL tells the computer to carry out a separate program.

This is useful as it allows the programming team to break a large program up into a number of smaller parts which can then be written and tested separately. When they are working they can then be joined together by allowing one program to CALL another.

Example (main program)

```
. . . .
PROCEDURE DIVISION.
PARA-1.
      CALL 'MESSAGE'
      STOP RUN.
```

In this example, the called program will be called *MESSAGE* on the disk directory.

Example (sub-program called 'message')

```
. . . .
PROCEDURE DIVISION.
PARA-1.
      DISPLAY 'HELLO'.
RETURN-TO-CALLING-PROG.
      EXIT PROGRAM.
```

Instead of STOP RUN, a sub-program should have the command   EXIT PROGRAM (to return to the main program).

The two programs can be compiled separately and then run.

Exercises
1.   Write two sub-programs - one of which will display the message 'Hello' on the screen and another which will display 'Goodbye'. Write a main program which will call each in turn - so that the two sets of messages appear on the screen in succession.
2.   Write a sub-program which will ask a user for his/her name and then say 'Hello' followed by the name. Write a main program which will call this routine 5 times. (Hint - put the CALL command within a paragraph which can then be PERFORMED .. TIMES).
3.   Write a sub-program which will display a screen full of asterisks. Call this routine from a main program.

88. Calling Sub-programs (2) -
Passing Parameters BY CONTENT

Two separate programs do not automatically have access to each other's data areas in memory. However, when a program calls a sub-program it may need to pass across information for the latter to use. The data items passed across in this way are known as *parameters*.

The following example (main) program asks a user how many stars he/she wants to display on the screen, then calls a sub-program and passes across the number required. The sub-program will then display the correct number of stars.

Example Main Program
```
. . . . . . .
DATA DIVISION.
WORKING-STORAGE SECTION.
01   NUMBER-OF-STARS      PIC   99.
PROCEDURE DIVISION.
GET-NUMBER-REQUIRED.
     DISPLAY 'HOW MAY STARS DO YOU WANT TO DISPLAY ?'
     ACCEPT NUMBER-OF-STARS.
DISPLAY-STARS.
     CALL 'SHOWSTAR' USING BY CONTENT NUMBER-OF-STARS.
```
The parameter NUMBER-OF-STARS is passed BY CONTENT which means that a copy of its contents will be transferred to the corresponding data item in the sub-program. The sub-program will not be able to access or alter the contents of the original data item.

```
FINAL-PARA.
     STOP RUN.
```


Example Sub-Program (called 'SHOWSTAR')
```
. . . . . . .
DATA DIVISION.
LINKAGE SECTION.
01   NUMBER-OF-ASTERISKS PIC   99.
```
The Linkage Section is placed after the Working-Storage Section if there is one.

```
PROCEDURE DIVISION USING NUMBER-OF-ASTERISKS.
```
NUMBER-OF-ASTERISKS will receive a copy of the contents of NUMBER-OF-STARS when the main program calls this sub-program.

Note that NUMBER-OF-ASTERISKS has to be defined in the Linkage Section of the Sub-program. The definition must not conflict with definition given to the related field in the main program (i.e. in length or type).

```
SHOW-ASTERISKS.
     PERFORM NUMBER-OF-ASTERISKS TIMES
          DISPLAY '*'
     END-PERFORM.

RETURN-TO-CALLING-PROG.
     EXIT PROGRAM.
```

89. Calling Sub-programs (3) -
Passing Parameters BY REFERENCE

A sub-program often has to pass information back to a main program.

The following example (main) program asks a student for his/her maths mark as a percentage then calls a sub-program which will work out the grade ('Pass' or 'Fail') and transfer this result back to the main program which will then display a report.

Example Main Program

```
...
DATA DIVISION.
WORKING-STORAGE SECTION.
01   MATHS-MARK     PIC 999.
01   MATHS-GRADE    PIC X(4).
PROCEDURE DIVISION.
GET-MARK.
     DISPLAY 'MATHS MARK ?'  ACCEPT MATHS-MARK.
DECIDE-GRADE.
     CALL 'GRADE' USING BY CONTENT MATHS-MARK,
                  BY REFERENCE MATHS-GRADE.
```

The mark is passed across by content - so the sub-program receives a copy of MATHS-MARK in a totally separate field called SUBJECT-MARK (as specified below) so it cannot alter the original field's contents.

However, the grade parameter is specified as BY REFERENCE which means that when the sub-program is called, the name SUBJECT-GRADE (as specified below) becomes (temporarily) just another name for exactly the field known as MATHS-GRADE to the main program. The sub-program will be able to modify the original field MATHS-GRADE automatically whenever it modifies SUBJECT-GRADE.

```
DISPLAY-REPORT.
     DISPLAY 'MATHS GRADE: ' MATHS-GRADE.
FINAL-PARA.
     STOP RUN.
```

Example Sub-Program

```
....
DATA DIVISION.
LINKAGE SECTION.
01   SUBJECT-MARK    PIC   999.
01   SUBJECT-GRADE   PIC   X(4).
PROCEDURE DIVISION USING SUBJECT-MARK, SUBJECT-GRADE.
```

The parameters have to be listed in the same order that the related items occur in the main program's CALL statement.

```
GRADE-ROUTINE.
     IF SUBJECT-MARK >= 50
     THEN
          MOVE 'PASS' TO SUBJECT-GRADE
     ELSE
          MOVE 'FAIL' TO SUBJECT-GRADE
     END-IF.
RETURN-TO-CALLING-PROG.
     EXIT PROGRAM.
```

90. Suggested Programming Projects

For each of the following projects - produce structure diagrams, a list of paragraph names to be used, a written version of the program before testing, a test plan and log, comments on any changes that were necessary to cure logic errors and a printout of the final correct version of the program.

1.   A library needs to store records of borrowers on disk which can be accessed quickly from a terminal as and when required.

Produce a program which makes use of an Indexed Sequential file to store the following information:

membership number	5 digits
surname	15 characters
first names	30 characters
address	60 characters
books on loan	space to store:
	code number (7 digits)
	and
	date due for return
	for 6 books.

The program should provide the following facilities via a menu:

a)   add a new member;
b)   change a members's details;
c)   print a list of all members;
d)   print a list of all members with overdue books
e)   print an individual reminder to each member with overdue books.

2.   Another library requires similar facilities but does not require immediate access to the information from terminals installed in the library. Instead, a list of additions and alterations to member's details will be listed on paper and typed in at the end of the day to a sequential transaction file. This, after sorting, will be used to update a sequential master file. The system will then automatically produce an up-to-date list of members and a list of all books that are overdue each night.

Produce the necessary programs to provide this system.